THE JOSHUA PRINCIPLE:

Fifty-two Scripture Verses
Every Believer Should Know

O.S. HAWKINS

The Joshua Principle:
Fifty-two Scripture Verses Every Believer Should Know
©2011 by O. S. Hawkins

Unless otherwise indicated, Scripture taken from the
HOLY BIBLE, NEW KING JAMES VERSION.˙

Library of Congress Cataloging-in-Publication Data
Hawkins, O. S.
The Joshua Principle: Fifty-two Scripture Verses
Every Believer Should Know / O.S. Hawkins.
Includes bibliographical references.
ISBN 978-0-9779400-6-6
1. Bible. Title.
BS2785.3.H39 1992
227.9107-dc20   92-17821

2011925940

Printed in the United States of America.
10 9 8 7 6 5 4 3 2 1

GuideStone®
Financial Resources

OTHER BOOKS BY O.S. HAWKINS

TABLE OF CONTENTS

ABOUT THE AUTHOR

 For more than 25 years, O.S. Hawkins served pastorates in Oklahoma, Florida and Texas. A native of Fort Worth, he has three earned degrees (BBA, MDiv and DMin) and several honorary degrees. He is president of GuideStone Financial Resources which serves 200,000 pastors, church staff members, missionaries, doctors, nurses, university professors and other workers of various Christian organizations with their retirement and benefit service needs. He is the author of more than 25 books and preaches regularly at Bible conferences, evangelism conferences and churches across the nation. He and his wife Susie have two married daughters and six grandchildren.

INTRODUCTION

Recently, while listening to our seven-year-old grand-child quote from memory an entire chapter of Psalms, it dawned upon me how few adults give thought, much less are intentional, as to the discipline of Scripture memory. What is "The Joshua Principle"? It is found in Joshua 1:8, "This Book of the Law shall not depart from your mouth, but you shall meditate on it day and night, that you may observe to do according to all that is written in it. For then you will make your way prosperous, and then you will have good success." The Joshua Principle is a challenge to keep the word in our mouths through memorization and to keep it in our hearts through meditation "day and night."

Many consistent Bible readers today seem to think it is the volume of Scripture they can devour daily that is most important. The 52 chapters in this volume are designed to lead the reader on a yearly journey by spending a week on one particular Scripture, memorizing it and meditating on it so that it is incarnated within and becomes a living part of our very being. The outlines in each chapter can also be used by the busy pastor or Bible teacher as a guide to challenge their hearers to a year of Scripture memory and meditation on the 52 verses every believer should know.

My own life was dramatically transformed when as a 17-year-old young man I came to know Christ as my own personal Savior and Lord. I could count on one hand the number of times I could recall being in a church service and did not even know Matthew, Mark, Luke or John were books of the Bible. The first week of my Christian experience someone handed me a slip of paper with 1 Corinthians 10:13 written on it. Then, looking me squarely in the face, said, "You better memorize this because you will need it!" Thus began a journey of Scripture memory which has served to lead me every day since. That verse says, "No temptation has overtaken you except such as is common to man; but God is faithful, who will not allow you to be tempted beyond what you are able, but with the temptation will make a way of escape, that you may be able to bear it." Only God knows how many times across the years I have arrived at temptation's corner and this verse, hidden in my heart and mind, came into my mouth and kept me on the right path.

Scripture memory enables us to take God's word with us anywhere and everywhere without carrying our Bibles. It enables us to receive the Word into our hearts, retain it in our minds and recall it in our mouths that we might speak it with power. This is exactly what our Lord did during his days of temptation in the wilderness of Judea. With each temptation Satan brought his way in Matthew 4, He answered with, "It is written…" The Word received and retained in our hearts and minds overcomes temptations when recalled in our mouths.

Scripture memory begins when we seek to understand the passage we are about to memorize. This is why there is an outline of the meaning of the passage accompanying every chapter in this volume. When memorizing Scripture, I have found it helpful to write it out in my own handwriting, phrase by phrase, on a small note card. I keep the card in my pocket throughout the day and week and numerous times during the day, while at my desk, at a stoplight in the car, or other such occasions, I simply review it until the first phrase is memorized, then the second and so on. It is helpful to me to quote the entire verse from memory upwards to a hundred times in order to "seal it" it my heart before going to another verse. Periodic review over the next few weeks is also essential.

Another important aspect of "The Joshua Principle" is to "meditate on it day and night." I sometimes wonder if fears of Eastern mysticism have robbed some Christians of the art of meditation. Webster defines mediation as "to engage in contemplation or reflection, to focus one's thoughts on: to reflect or ponder over." Or, as the Bible says, "Think on these things." This is exactly what Mary, the young teenage virgin girl from Nazareth, did when she received the word that she was pregnant and when her child was born. She "kept all these things and pondered them in her heart" (Luke 2:19). She meditated, "pondered," upon these things. The Greek word here is a compound word meaning "to stir together" just as a cook would put different ingredients into a pot and stir them, simmer them together. This was the essence of the Psalmist's plea in Psalm 19:14 when he said, "Let the words of my mouth and the meditations of my heart be acceptable in your sight, O Lord, my strength and my Redeemer." One of the disciplines I have found personally helpful in meditation is to repeat the verse again and again putting the inflection on a different word each time. It is amazing how much insight comes from this simple practice.

God's Word is powerful and profitable when studied and applied by anyone; the young and the seasoned believer alike. The early church father, Augustine, said, "God's Word is shallow enough not to drown the young, but deep enough that the greatest theologian will never touch the bottom."

Thus we begin our journey on the way to making "The Joshua Principle" a daily part of our lives as we recover the beauty of Scripture memory and meditation. Yes, "this Book of the Law shall not depart from your mouth, but you shall meditate in it day and night, that you may observe to do according to all that is written in it. For then you will make your way prosperous, and then you will have good success." There are 52 verses every believer should know by memory. Let's begin the journey with the first verse of the entire Bible.

CHAPTER 1:
Everyone Has a Worldview

> *"In the beginning God created the heavens*
> *and the earth" (Genesis 1:1).*

Everyone has a worldview. We all view life through some type of lens. Certain predisposed persuasions or, seemingly, benign biases do, in fact, determine how each of us views our world. Presently, the Western world is engaged in a huge confrontation between competing worldviews. I spent my boyhood years in the 1950s when the Judeo-Christian worldview was front and center in prominence in America. Our young men and women had just returned from the European Theatre or the South Pacific at the conclusion of World War II. They married their high school sweethearts and began what sociologists now call the great baby boom. We were a thankful and grateful people. Church attendance was at an all-time high and Bible readings were everyday occurrences in public schools. We viewed our world through a modern, yet moralistic, lens.

My teenage years were spent in the 1960s. The assassination of President John F. Kennedy ushered in that decade and something happened to the psyche of America. We became more introspective in our worldview. It began to be reflected in the music of the day. Peter, Paul and Mary sang, "The answer, my friend, is blowing in the wind." Suddenly our introspection revealed that the simple answers we thought we held were now questioned. Our worldview began to subtly change. For many, the answers to life's questions which they thought they held seemed to be "blowing in the wind."

Then came the 1970s ushered in on the throws of Watergate, Roe vs. Wade and Vietnam. The culture became more skeptical. Again, it was reflected in the music of the day. Billy Joel's big hit in those days was "Only the good die young." Skepticism became the lens by which many in our culture began to view their world. This was followed by a bit of a reprieve in the 1980s. Ronald Reagan brought a new hope as he spoke about that "shining city on a hill." Then came the 1990s. The Berlin Wall fell; the Cold War came to a sudden conclusion. Next, the new millennium was ushered in on the heels of September 11, 2001, and the War on Terror was launched with a significant effect upon the worldview of many.

However, even though worldviews may change across the decades, there is a single constant that does not change. The simple fact is that one's worldview can be determined by one's response to the first four words of the Bible: "In the beginning God…" If we believe these four words, then we will view our world through the lens of Scripture which does not change. If we do not, then we will continue to view our world through the lens of culture which continuously changes.

Perhaps there is no other verse under such constant abuse and ridicule as Genesis 1:1. It demands the answer to three important questions. **When? Who? What?**

WHEN? *(In the beginning)*

It should be noted that history does not begin in Genesis 1:1 but back before it, way back in the eternal councils of God. There we find three things: love, glory and eternal life.

Before Genesis 1:1, there was love. In His high intercessory prayer, the Lord Jesus prayed, "Father, I desire that they also whom You gave Me, may be with Me where I am, that they may behold My glory which you have given Me; for You loved Me before the foundation of the world." (John 17:24). Before the foundation of the world in Genesis 1:1, there was love.

Back in the eternal recesses of God, before Genesis 1:1, there also existed glory. Earlier in that same prayer, Jesus had prayed, "And now, O Father, glorify Me together with Yourself, with the glory which I had with You before the world was." (John 17:5). Long before what we refer to as the "beginning," the glory of God existed.

There also existed the promise of eternal life back before the "beginning." The Apostle Paul writing to Titus, inspired by the Holy Spirit Himself, penned it thus, "In hope of eternal life which God, who cannot lie, promised before time began" (Titus 1:2). Our hope of eternal life and its promise was there before "time began," before "the beginning."

One should not think of Genesis 1:1 as the beginning of everything for, as John begins his gospel, "In the beginning was the Word and the Word was with God, and the Word was God." So that there be no mistake about whom he spoke, he added, "And the Word became flesh and dwelt among us, and we beheld His glory, the glory as of the only begotten of the Father, full of grace and truth." (John 1:1, 14).

WHO? *(God)*

The Bible translates the Hebrew, *Elohim*, here for "God." The significance is that it is in its plural form. It is a plural noun thus hinting to us in the initial verse of Scripture that God is one person pictured in three, Father, Son and Holy Spirit. Interestingly, the verb, "created," which follows this noun, is in the singular form, seemingly making a mockery of linguistic grammar. Yet, it should be singular in that He is the great Three in One. We see this truth revealed later in Genesis 1 when we read, "Let *Us* make man in *Our* own image" (Genesis 1:26). And then the following verse reads, "So God created man in *His* own image." (Genesis 1:27).

The doctrine of the trinity is one of the great mysteries of the Bible. Yet, beginning with this first verse, the idea of the trinity is woven throughout the Scripture. It is often illustrated by the nature of H_2O; two parts hydrogen and one part oxygen. We all know this to be water, a liquid. However, it can also be a solid (ice) or a vapor (steam). Yet, in all three manifestations it is still the same nature, H_2O. And so it is with God manifesting Himself in three persons.

WHAT? *(Created the heavens and the earth)*

There is a huge difference between "creating" something and "making" something. Many of us have made many things. But, none of us has ever created anything from nothing. A cabinet maker may make a beautiful cabinet out of wood. However, he is totally unable to create the wood itself. The Hebrew word which we translate, "created," in this verse carries with it the connotation that something is created out of nothing.

This physical universe was spoken into existence by God Himself. Is it possible that the entire vast expanse "above" us; the solar systems, the constellations, and the measureless space, all having billions of stars moving in clocklike precision, do so without a master creator and designer? Is it possible that no one else among the billions of people presently on the planet has a "DNA" or thumbprint quite like yours? Is that possible without Someone behind it all Who sees you as indescribably valuable to Himself?

As you memorize this verse this week, meditate on the depth behind each of these sacred words and remember that these first four words of the Bible determine one's own personal worldview. Yes, indeed, "In the beginning God…!" Make these four words the lens through which you view your world.

CHAPTER 2:
The Most Often Quoted Verse in the Bible

"For God so loved the world that He gave His only begotten Son, that whoever believes in Him should not perish but have everlasting life" (John 3:16).

If we ever memorized a verse of Scripture, it is most likely John 3:16. It is the verse most often heard in the simplicity and beauty of a little child's voice proudly reciting it from memory. It is the one verse showing up on large placards at football games and other major sporting events. Those signs are located where television cameras cannot avoid its message. This is the one verse that has escaped the lips of many older saints as they breathed their final breath. It is the entire gospel in a nutshell.

The late evangelist, Angel Martinez (who had memorized the entire New Testament), referred to John 3:16 as salvation's formula. It is the gospel in one verse. And indeed it is. It reveals to us salvation's cause, its cost, its condition and its consequence.

SALVATION'S CAUSE (*"For God so loved the world"*)

The motivating factor behind God's redemptive plan for every man and woman is found in His love for us. He not only loves us. He "SO" loves us! Later, the Apostle Paul would seek to describe this love by speaking of its "breadth, length, depth and height." "God is love" and this deep emotion is what brings about the possibility of our redemption; knowing Him in the intimacy of Father and child. God's love for you is the motivating cause of salvation. "For God SO loved…"

SALVATION'S COST
("that He gave His only begotten Son")

Our salvation, the free pardoning of our sin and the promise of abundant and eternal life in Christ, did not come without cost. Freedom is never free. It is always bought with blood. From the early chapters of Genesis, there is a "Scarlet Thread" woven throughout the pages of Scripture revealing the blood atonement. It climaxes in the final and complete sacrifice for sin on a Roman cross outside the city gates of Jerusalem. Jesus not only spoke of His love for us, but, He "demonstrated His own love toward us in that while we were still sinners, Christ died for us" (Romans 5:8). Our salvation in Christ came at a great cost, "He gave His only begotten Son."

SALVATION'S CONDITION
("that whosoever believes in Him")

Salvation is not spelled "d-o" but "d-o-n-e." Many think their own good works are the pathway to eternal life. Consequently, they do this or do that or they don't do this or don't do that all in order to earn salvation. But our salvation is "done." It is already purchased for us with the blood of

Christ on the Cross. Our part is to "believe," to transfer our trust from ourselves and our own efforts to His finished work on the cross of Calvary.

To believe does not mean to simply give intellectual assent to the claims of Christ. It means to transfer our trust to Him alone for our salvation. The most pointed question in the entire Bible is asked of the Apostle Paul by a Philippian jailor, "What must I do to be saved?" (Acts 16:30). Paul's pointed reply immediately follows in the next verse, "Believe on the Lord Jesus Christ and you will be saved…" I believe "in" George Washington, but I don't believe "on" him, I don't trust my life to Him. Salvation's condition is through faith and faith alone in the finished work of the Lord Jesus Christ.

SALVATION'S CONSEQUENCE
("shall not perish but have everlasting life")

What a consequence! What a promise! Those without Christ are "perishing." But, those in Christ have the eternal promise of "everlasting life. " This comes not from our own human efforts, morals or good deeds, but the promise is to those who realize that God's love reaches down to us, was made possible by a great price, and is received by grace through faith alone; believing on the Lord Jesus Christ.

An unknown, yet wise, old sage once quoted John 3:16 as following:

> *For God…the greatest lover*
> *So loved…the greatest degree*

The world. . .the greatest company
That He gave. . .the greatest act
His only begotten Son. . .the greatest gift
That whoever. . .the greatest opportunity
Believes. . .the greatest simplicity
In Him. . .the greatest attraction
Should not perish. . .the greatest promise
But. . .the greatest difference
Have. . .the greatest certainty
Everlasting life. . .the greatest possession.

As you memorize this old and oft-repeated verse this week, meditate on the fact that love is always something you do and remember that "God so loved the world that He gave." Yes, God knows you, loves you and has a wonderful plan for your life.

CHAPTER 3:
Amazing Grace

"For by grace you have been saved through faith, and that not of yourselves; it is the gift of God" (Ephesians 2:8).

Christianity has always been cross-cultural. Its message transcends the various cultures of the world. Its roots were in a first-century Middle Eastern Jewish culture. Later it deeply impacted a sophisticated European culture. Then, it continued to spread westward and became the basis of a New World culture. Today it is growing exponentially in an Eastern culture.

The modern church sometimes forgets that the Christian faith is not simply cross-cultural, but has also, and always, been counter-cultural as well. Western culture today is telling us in a thousand ways that there are many different roads which lead to eternal life. Many contend we are all going to the same place, just simply getting there by different paths. However, the Bible reminds us that "there is a way that seems right to a man, but its end is the way of death" (Proverbs 14:12). Salvation is entirely God's work, in God's way, according to God's will.

SALVATION IS GOD'S WORK
("By grace you have been saved")

Where does our salvation have its origin? Many today

believe it is the work of man; that one can merit good favor by one's own good deeds. But Christianity is counter-cultural. It began way back in the eternal councils of God in eternity past. Earlier in this Ephesian letter, the Apostle Paul says, "He chose us in Him before the foundation of the world, that we should be holy and without blame before Him in love" (Ephesians 1:4). Salvation is God's work.

Our salvation is "by grace" and not in response to any good works which we may, or may not, have done. It is provided for us wholly due to His "grace;" His unmerited and undeserved favor. The Father did not send the Lord Jesus to die for our sin because we kept begging and pleading with Him to do so. It was by His grace alone. There is a difference in mercy and grace. Mercy is not getting what we do deserve. Grace is getting what we do not deserve. No wonder we call it "amazing."

SALVATION IS GOD'S WORK IN GOD'S WAY
("through faith…not of yourselves…the gift of God)

When I read this verse I find myself wanting to shout those words, "Through Faith…not of yourselves…it is the gift of God!" And, in the context, the following verse continues, "Not of works lest anyone should boast" (Ephesians 2:9). Scripture says our salvation is by grace and through faith; that is, trusting in God alone. The Greek preposition preceding the word, "faith," indicates that our faith is the channel through which our salvation flows from God to us.

It is "through" faith. In Israel archeologists have uncovered an ancient aqueduct through which the Romans brought their fresh water from the Carmel Mountains in the north down to the port city of Caesarea. It stands today as a reminder, a word picture, of how our own faith is the aqueduct through which the living water of God's saving grace flows to us.

Paul's repetition of this truth that salvation is "not of yourselves" and "not of works" emphasizes the point. Go to India today and the religion of the masses will reveal some followers pulling wagons with giant hooks in their backs; others lying on beds of nails, and still others plunging into the Ganges River. All of this being done in a feeble attempt to appease the Almighty. But, it is "by faith…not of yourselves…it is the gift of God." Certain followers of Islam today rush out to die in Jihad in hopes of being ushered immediately into heaven and being welcomed by dozens of virgins. In Latin America one can find those during the Holy Days crawling on their knees up rocky paths to the top of mountains, to be nailed to crosses, all in their morbid search for penance. But it is "by faith…not of yourselves…it is the gift of God."

There are only two religions in our world: true religion and false religion. One is a religion of works while the other is freely obtained "by grace through faith." No amount of human effort, good deeds or giving of our resources can buy God's favor. And what amazes me is that God is freely offering this incredible gift, and we still have to encourage and exhort people to receive it. Salvation is God's work (by grace) in God's way (by faith).

SALVATION IS GOD'S WORK IN GOD'S WAY ACCORDING TO GOD'S WILL

The eighth and ninth verses of the second chapter of Paul's letter to the Ephesians cannot stand alone without finding themselves within the context of verse ten. "For we are His workmanship, created in Christ Jesus for good works, which God prepared beforehand that we should walk in them" (Ephesians 2:10). This is an awesome thought — "We are His workmanship." We actually get our English word "poem" from the Greek word which translates "workmanship." You are God's special creation, his own work of art. He so fashioned and formed you that no one else has a DNA like yours. You are unique to Him and indescribably valuable. You are His workmanship, His own special work of art.

The believer is a new creation. He is "created in Christ Jesus." Paul, in his letter to the Corinthians, addresses this very fact saying, "If anyone is in Christ, he is a new creation; old things have passed away; behold, all things have become new" (2 Corinthians 5:17). Christians are not men and women who have been improved upon because they took on a new set of moral standards. They are "new creations in

Christ Jesus;" His own special "poem." Thus, the Christian life is not simply a changed life but an exchanged life.

And, all this was "prepared beforehand" by God Himself "that we should walk" with Him. Not only is this salvation His work and in His way, but it is also according to His will.

As you memorize this valuable verse this week, meditate on the fact that God has made a way out of no way for any and all who will come to Him by faith alone in His finished work of redemption. And, it is all because of His "Amazing Grace!" Yes, salvation is God's work in God's way according to God's will.

CHAPTER 4:
A Psalm for the Ages

"The LORD is my shepherd; I shall not want" (Psalm 23:1).

Virtually every educated mind in the English speaking world has heard the words of this Psalm of King David. Some of our earliest recollections are associated with these poetic passages. It is as though it never grows old. In fact, often when we come before it, we continue to find new meaning. Like John 3:16, these words have silently escaped the lips of many a soldier under a star filled sky during a dark night in a foxhole on some far away battlefield. These are the words that are formed from the dying lips of many on their beds of affliction. These words, like a lullaby for fear, have brought hope and peace to millions across the centuries.

Before David was ever a king, he was a shepherd boy in the fields of Bethlehem. Later in life, as he penned this "Shepherd's Psalm," he reflected on those days with his sheep. Only a shepherd could have penned the depth of meaning we find in the six short verses which make up the Twenty-third Psalm.

One should read slowly these first five words of the Psalm. "The—Lord—is—my—shepherd." Those five words hold the key and form the foundation to the entire Psalm. Once sealed in our own hearts, these words tell us much about our relationship with this good and great Shepherd.

HE IS PREEMINENT *("THE Lord is my shepherd")*

The Scripture does not say, "A Lord is my shepherd." It says, "THE Lord is my shepherd." There is no other Lord. He has no peer. You speak of Washington and I can speak of Lincoln. You speak of Beethoven and I can speak of Handel. You speak of Alexander and I can speak of Napoleon. But, when it comes to Christ, He stands alone and without peer. There is only one Lord! The Hebrew word translated "Lord" here in Psalm 23 is "Yahweh." The Jews rendered this name so holy, and stood in such awe of it, they would not even speak it publicly.

Only the records of heaven have recorded how many martyrs in the early church went to their deaths and laid down their lives because of the insistence of these first two words in this Psalm, "The Lord." They would neither bow nor bend to profess Caesar as Lord. They gave their lives because they were convinced there was only one Lord and His sweet name was Jesus. Our God is still preeminent. He is THE, one and only, Lord.

HE IS PRESENT *("The Lord IS my shepherd)*

Oh, the depth of meaning for us in this little two-letter word. This great preeminent Lord is with me right now. "The Lord IS my shepherd." This is not past tense. It does not say, "The Lord was my shepherd." It is not future tense. It does not say, "The Lord will be my shepherd." He is pres-

The Joshua Principle: *Fifty-Two Scripture Verses Every Believer Should Know*   **33**

ent — "The Lord IS my shepherd." He is with us this very moment to meet our present needs.

Earlier, on the backside of an Egyptian desert, God called Moses from a burning bush to become the great emancipator of his people. When he briefly balked at going back to Pharaoh, he asked God who he should say had sent him. God replied, "I AM WHO I AM...thus you shall say... I AM has sent me to you." (Exodus 3:14). Unlike the other world religions, we do not have a leader who has long since departed the scene or one who is still yet to come. He is the great "I AM" and not the great "I WAS," or, the great "I WILL BE." No wonder David said, "The Lord IS my shepherd." David would reinforce this in the initial verse of Psalm 46 by saying, "God is our refuge and strength, a very present help in time of trouble."

HE IS PERSONAL *("The Lord is MY shepherd")*

There is a huge difference in saying, "The Lord is A shepherd" and saying, "The Lord is MY shepherd." What a difference comes to life's circumstances and situations with that little word, "My." We may hear of someone's child who is deathly sick, and we have compassion and feel sorrow. But what a difference it makes if it is "my" child. This is not just any shepherd about whom the Psalmist speaks. This is MY shepherd.

This small two-letter word is an awesome addition to the text. We are not simply insignificant specks of protoplasm in this vast array of solar systems. The fact that the God of this universe is concerned for me personally gives purpose and meaning to my short sojourn on this small planet hung in His vast expanse. Oh, the thought of it…He is MY shepherd!

Unfortunately, however, not everyone can say this. Our faith must be personal in order to know Him. Those who have placed their trust in Christ know Him in the intimacy of Father and child and Shepherd and sheep. Jesus said it thus, "My sheep hear My voice, and I know them, and they follow Me. And I give them eternal life, and they shall never perish; neither shall anyone snatch them out of My hand" (John 10:27-28). Christ's sheep know His voice and they follow Him. He is personal. He is MY shepherd.

HE IS PROTECTIVE *("The Lord is my SHEPHERD")*

One thousand years after King David penned these words there stood one who said, "I am the Good Shepherd. The Good Shepherd gives His life for the sheep." (John 10:11). When we read Psalm 23, we are reading about this Great Shepherd Savior.

Our shepherd is protective. This is the very nature of a shepherd. Without a good shepherd, the sheep could not find their way to water or to other of life's necessities. The shepherd keeps a constant vigil for wild animals or other dangers which might harm his sheep. The good shepherd goes after the sheep which stray from the fold. Could one ever forget the story Jesus told of the lost sheep in Luke 15? Without a shepherd sheep are virtually helpless. They could not find their way through treacherous mountain passes, run fast enough to escape a predator, nor are they strong enough to defend themselves. In fact, sheep are not prepared for flight or fight. Just as sheep need a shepherd, so do we have need of our shepherd. Yes, "The Lord is my shepherd."

A final thought…if you have ever observed a shepherd with his sheep, you have observed an insightful lesson. The shepherd is always out in front of the sheep; never behind them. Shepherds lead sheep, they do not drive them as cattlemen do their cattle. The shepherd leads and the sheep follow. Our Lord will never force us or drive us against our will. However, He will lead us. All we have to do is follow. We can trust that One who has "given His life for His sheep."

It might be that this week you will want to memorize all six verses of Psalm 23. And, as you do, meditate on the fact that our great God is preeminent, present, personal and protective. Yes, "The—LORD—is—my—shepherd."

CHAPTER 5:
The Family Secret

> *"And we know that all things work together for*
> *good to those who love God, to those who are the called*
> *according to His purpose" (Romans 8:28).*

Anyone who has been raised within a family environment has his or her own share of family secrets. These little tid-bits of reality are usually best kept within the small circle of family. For some these family secrets are dark and hidden in the back recesses of the mind. For most of us, they are filled with light, spontaneous, perhaps a bit embarrassing and, often, downright funny.

Did you know that those of us who have been born into God's family also have a family secret? There is something that we know that those who are not part of God's forever family do not know. Our family secret is found in our verse for this week, Romans 8:28. On numerous occasions across my own Christian pilgrimage, I have climbed up on top of this verse and found refuge and hope in times of confusion or need. There are four factors related to "the family secret" which every believer should know.

IT IS CONFIDENTIAL *("And WE know…")*

Note carefully this plural pronoun, "We." Yes, we know. This verse is not intended to be understood by the world. To the lost person these words are folly and even foolishness. They cannot be understood. Why? This is our family secret… "We know!" This verse only applies to true believers. Confront the existentialist today who seems to see no real purpose in history. He has no hopeful explanation for sudden death, sickness or various set-backs in life. The Christian comes along and says, "Yes, there is, but it is a family secret…AND WE KNOW that all things work together for good to those who love God, to those who are called according to His purpose."

Interestingly, the Bible translates our English word, "know," from a Greek word which means that we don't even have to know experientially here. It is just a stated fact; we just know intuitively. We have a family secret within God's family and it is confidential. "We know!"

IT IS CONSTRUCTIVE
("…things work together for good…")

This is one of the most comforting thoughts in all of Scripture. Things that happen in life have a way of working together for our good. They are constructive. As we each look back over our Christian experience, how many events which we may have thought at the time were disastrous, actually, in the end, worked out for good? Yes, "things work together," neither by accident nor blind chance. God, Himself, is behind the scenes in each of our lives.

One Greek word translates this entire phrase in the

language of the New Testament. We get our word, "synergy," by transliterating this ancient word. There is a constructive and synergistic principle at work in our family secret. This certainly does not mean that everything that happens is good. In fact, many are confronted with things that are bad. There are financial failings, sicknesses, disappointments, ad infinitum. However, it does mean that God can take our mistakes and our messes and work them together for our own good. King David realized this and recorded these poignant words for all posterity, "It was good for me that I have been afflicted, that I may learn your statutes." (Psalm 119:71). As believers, we have a very special family secret which is confidential and constructive.

IT IS COMPREHENSIVE
("...ALL THINGS work together for good...")

When I meditate on these words I am prone to ask myself, "Can I really believe this?" Had the Apostle Paul said, "some things" or "many things" or even, "most things" it would be a bit more palatable. But, "all things?" All things may include unfair things. This was certainly true for Joseph who was sold into slavery and later falsely accused of a crime which landed him in an Egyptian prison. All things may include difficult things. This was certainly true of Paul who was shipwrecked at Malta, stoned at Lystra and left for dead, beaten and berated across the years of his missionary journeys. He knew well, from firsthand experience, what the Holy Spirit led him to write when he penned these words of our family secret.

Yes, all things are what? Working together. For what? Good. For example, I would not like to sit down to a meal to eat a bowl of baking soda. In, and of, itself it is distasteful. Nor, would I look forward to eating a nice serving of flour. However, put them together, add a few more other ingredients, stir them up, put them in the oven, and I can attest to the fact that I love biscuits! All things, not necessarily in and of themselves, but when worked together in the tapestry of the cross, come out for our good and for God's glory. This family secret is not only constructive, it is comprehensive. Yes, all things are working together for our good this very moment.

IT IS CONDITIONAL *("...to those who love God, to those who are the called according to His purpose.")*

An unofficial poll taken of Sunday morning church attendees asked them to quote Romans 8:28. The majority of them left off the first phrase, "And we know." They simply began with the phrase, "All things work together for good..." But, interestingly, they also left off the last phrase which states, "to those who love God, to those who are the called according to His purpose."

Our family secret is conditional. It is not a blanket, unconditional promise for everyone. It is for those who "love God." Those who do not love Him are generally resentful at certain things which may come their way. Only those who love Him and sense that there is purpose in their lives can understand the deep truth of Romans 8:28 and say with Job, "Naked I came from my mother's womb, and naked shall I return there. The Lord gave, and the Lord has taken away; blessed be the name of the Lord." (Job 1:21).

Love is something we do. In the Bible, it is always equated with action. Jesus said, "If you love me, keep my commandments" (John 14:15). John framed it by saying we can know that we love God "when we keep His commandments." (I John 5:3). Thus, we come to the bottom-line questions. Do we love God? Do we sense that we are called to His purpose for our lives? Loving God and abiding in His will (His purpose) is the condition by which the truth of this verse comes home to our hearts.

As you memorize this verse this week, meditate on the deep reality that God is awake and aware of everything which may come our way. He has His own wonderful way of turning our bitterness into blessing. We have a "family secret" in God's forever family.

CHAPTER 6:
Being Comes Before Doing

"Blessed are those who hunger and thirst for righteousness,
for they shall be filled" (Matthew 5:6).

The Lord began His famous Sermon on the Mount with a series of verses that have come to be known as the Beatitudes. Our verse for this week is planted squarely in the middle of this section. All the beatitudes coming before it point to it. And, all of the ones following it issue out of it. It is important to understand what our Lord is driving home here. These are the "Be"-attitudes and not the "Do"-attitudes. Being comes before doing for what we do is always determined by who we are.

The Beatitudes are not a set of rules, such as the Ten Commandments, by which we are to live. The Ten Commandments have to do with actions. The Beatitudes have to do with attitudes. The Ten Commandments have to do with conduct. The Beatitudes have to do with character. Why is it so imperative that we believers incarnate these beatitudes into our very being? It is because our actions flow from our attitudes and our conduct issues out of our character. Let's take a journey down this pathway toward the Spirit-controlled life.

THE PATHWAY TOWARD THE LIFE OF BLESSING *(Matthew 5:3-5)*

This pathway begins with the first Beatitude, "Blessed are the poor in spirit, for theirs is the kingdom of heaven" (Matthew 5:3). There is no premium to be found in poverty here. Note these are the poor in "spirit." That is, blessed are the ones who realize their total abject poverty, spiritually speaking, apart from the Lord Jesus Christ.

The next step along this pathway is found in the second Beatitude, "Blessed are those who mourn, for they shall be comforted" (Matthew 5:4). It is not enough to simply realize that without Christ we are poverty stricken spiritually. Blessing emanates from the fact that we are burdened by it, grieved at our spiritual condition and actually mourn over the fact. Isaiah got to this place and exclaimed, "Woe is me!" Job said, "I abhor myself." Peter said, "Depart from me, Lord, for I am a sinful man."

The final step in this pathway is found in the next Beatitude, "Blessed are the meek, for they shall inherit the earth" (Matthew 5:5). The word picture of this Greek word, which we translate into English as "meek," is of an animal that has been domesticated. For example, it is a wild stallion which is ridden and "broken" by a cowboy so that it begins to go, turn or stop with a slight move of the bridle's reins. The stallion's will has been broken to the master's will. And so it is with the believer who knows something of the spirit-controlled life. First, he realizes that without Christ, he is poverty stricken spiritually. This brings a burden to his heart and he mourns over his spiritual neglect. This is followed by his coming under the control of his Master, such that his will is lost in his Master's will. Thus, we join Jesus in His Gethsemane plea, "Not my will but yours be done."

THE PASSAGEWAY INTO THE LIFE OF BLESSING *(Matthew 5:6)*

Now we arrive at the passageway into the life of blessing at the fourth beatitude, "Blessed are those who hunger and thirst for righteousness, for they shall be filled" (Matthew 5:6). It is not those who are hungering and thirsting after happiness who are being satisfied. It is those who strive for the righteousness of Christ in their own lives. The real irony is that the satisfied ones are not those who have arrived at righteousness but those who "hunger and thirst" for it. There is a paradoxical principle in play here. The believer is one who is hungering and thirsting and at the same time being filled in the very process.

At my former church there was a large ministry to the homeless people of our city. As many as 400 beds housed multitudes of men and women each night, and on some days many times more than that were fed hot meals. I noticed something about men who were truly hungry. I would watch them as they stood in line to enter the building. A hungry man is a humble man. Many a man stood in that line, perhaps a dirty ball cap rolled up in his hands, as he waited for a meal with his head bowed in humility. Jesus said, "Blessed are those who hunger and thirst for righteousness, for they shall be filled." Those being filled with God's best are those who are hungering and thirsting for the things of God with a humble spirit.

THE PROOFS ISSUING OUT OF THE LIFE OF BLESSING *(Matthew 5:7-10)*

If the first three beatitudes show us the pathway and the middle one shows us the passageway, then the final beatitudes reveal the proof that one is living the Spirit-controlled life. The first proof is found here, "Blessed are the merciful, for they shall obtain mercy" (Matthew 5:7). Having received mercy in our thirst for righteousness, our first reaction is to show mercy to those who around us. Show me someone who is hungering for righteousness, and I will show you someone who is showing mercy. On the other hand, show me someone who has no mercy on others, and I will show you someone who has not walked down the pathway to blessing much less entered its passageway.

The next proof is found in these words, "Blessed are the pure in heart, for they shall see God" (Matthew 5:8). It becomes as natural as water running downhill for the man who is pursuing God to have a pure heart in motives and morals. The third proof is found in the next beatitude, "Blessed are the peacemakers, for they shall be called sons of God" (Matthew 5:9). Note that Christ pronounces a blessing here on the "peacemakers" and not the "peace lovers."

These are the active promoters of unity among the family of God. And note they are not made sons of God by this outward manifestation, but they are "called" sons of God. They are recognized by others as such. Show me someone who tries to sow seeds of discord, and I will show you someone who is not thirsting for the things of God. On the other hand, show me someone who is after God's heart, and I will show you someone living in love and unity with those around him. As we meditate on these words of Christ, we should be asking ourselves, "Am I extending mercy even to those who may not be deserving? Is my heart pure? Am I a promoter of love and unity with those around me?"

Finally, Jesus says, "Blessed are those who are persecuted for righteousness' sake, for theirs is the kingdom of heaven" (Matthew 5:10). Show me someone who is never confronted with spiritual obstacles, and I will show you someone not hungry for the things of God. If we are not meeting the devil head on from time to time, we are most likely going the same way he is headed! One of the proofs of the Spirit-controlled life is often spiritual confrontation and even conflict "for righteousness sake."

It is interesting to note that these beatitudes begin in verse 3 and end in verse 10 with the same promise, "For theirs is the kingdom of heaven." Could this be God's subtle way of reminding us that "our citizenship is in heaven," that although we live and interact here in this physical plane, we are, in fact, members of another kingdom, one that lasts throughout the endless ages of eternity?

As you memorize this verse this week, meditate on the fact that God has a life of blessing for you, and remember that being comes before doing for what we do is always determined by who we are. Or, in the believer's case, whose we are! Yes, "Blessed are those who hunger and thirst for righteousness, for they shall be filled."

CHAPTER 7:
God's Remedy for Man's Sin

> *"All we like sheep have gone astray; we have turned, every one, to his own way; and the Lord has laid on Him the iniquity of us all" (Isaiah 53:6).*

In the early chapters of Genesis, when God took the skin of an innocent, sacrificial animal and covered the nakedness of Adam and Eve, the sun of God's redemptive revelation concerning Christ and the cross began to rise. Thus, the Old Testament shadows of the cross began to emerge. Among these shadows is found the revealing encounter of Abraham's sacrifice of his son, Isaac, in Genesis 22. Here we see the pointed picture of the coming substitutionary death of Christ with the ram which took Isaac's place on the altar of sacrifice. This revelatory sun continued its ascent as we arrive at Exodus 12 and are introduced to the revealing story of the Passover Lamb, without blemish and spot. The blood of this sacrifice provided two things for the ancient Israelites; deliverance from death and freedom from slavery. As the sun of this revelation continues to rise, it casts a perfect shadow of the coming Messiah when it arrives at Isaiah 53. This is one of the mountaintops of Scripture and the most perfect shadow, the most vivid and vibrant picture of the Lord Jesus, to be found in the Old Testament.

Recently, while meditating upon Isaiah 53:6, I was captured by the first phrase, "All we like sheep." This metaphorical expression is used repeatedly throughout Scripture. One can never come to understand the deep meaning of this passage without gleaning an insight as to how it is that we resemble these woolly creatures, so dependent upon their shepherd for their survival. There are several principles in play here which merit our inquiry.

SHEEP ARE DUMB

Think about it. Have you ever been to a circus? If so, you most likely saw an array of trained animals. Huge elephants can be trained to stand on their back legs upon tiny stools. Monkeys can be trained to ride bicycles around in a small circle. Lions can be trained to jump through rings of fire. But, have you ever seen a trained sheep? No. Sheep are dumb; they cannot be trained to do anything. They tend to wander around and frequently become lost because they simply follow their appetite with their heads down.

It is no wonder the prophet says, "All we like sheep have gone astray." Most people are opinionated. They talk profusely about politics, sports and the like. However, if you want to hear an unintelligent conversation from the mouths of semi-intelligent people, get them into a conversation about God's plan of redemption and His remedy for sin. How ignorant are so many when it comes to life's greatest subject? Yes, we are more like sheep than some of us might want to admit.

SHEEP ARE DIRECTIONLESS

Sheep tend to simply wander and meander aimlessly along the hillsides. They have no sense of direction. This is not true with other animals. When I was a boy, our family pet was a dog by the name of Penny. On a given day she followed several older boys in the neighborhood as they rode their bicycles to a lake over 10 miles from our home. Late in the afternoon they returned... without her. More than three weeks later while eating dinner in our home, I heard a familiar scratching on the backdoor. I opened the door and to my surprise there was my little dog, somewhat mangy and thin, but home at last. Many animals have an inner instinct that enables them to find their way home from great distances. But not sheep, they are directionless.

Yes, "All we like sheep have gone astray." So many men and women go through life without any real sense of direction, void of any perceived purpose. Many simply exist and have never learned how to live because, "like sheep," they have no sense of direction in life.

SHEEP ARE DEFENSELESS

Most every animal has some type of defense mechanism. Rabbits can run. Cats can scratch. Dogs can bite. Porcupines can puncture. Bees can sting. Goats can butt. Skunks...well, you get the point. But sheep? They are defenseless. They are totally unprepared for fight or for flight. They cannot fight other animals and they cannot out run those who seek them for prey. They are virtually helpless and void of any type of defense.

The man without the Lord Jesus Christ is like a sheep. He is helpless to get to the fold himself. He is on his own against "the wiles of the devil;" ill equipped for fight or flight.

Since we find ourselves "like sheep," dumb, directionless and defenseless; and since "we have turned, every one, to his own way," God has come to our rescue. "And the Lord has laid on Him (Jesus) the iniquity of us all." There is no clearer explanation of what transpired on the cross of Calvary than in these words of Isaiah 53:6. On the cross the Lord Jesus took our sin in His own body, bearing the wrath of God's punishment we deserved. He suffered the hurt, the humiliation of our sin, the agony and the death we deserved to die. He died our death so that we could live His life. He took our sin so that we could take His righteousness. Not only was His death on the cross voluntary, but it was vicarious. He died in my place. What a Savior!

As you memorize this verse this week, meditate on the fact that "God demonstrated His own love toward us in that while we were still sinners Christ died for us." (Romans 5:8). God does not have simply "a" remedy, but the "only" remedy for our sin. "All we like sheep have gone astray...we have turned everyone to his own way...and the Lord has laid upon Him the iniquity of us all."

CHAPTER 8:
Three Levels of Prayer

"Ask, and it will be given to you; seek, and you will find; knock, and it will be opened to you" (Matthew 7:7).

While Scripture memory and meditation is vital to a victorious Christian life, the same can be said for a vibrant and virtuous prayer life. God speaks to us through His Word and we speak to Him through our prayers of praise, petition and intercession. Without the Bible, prayer has no real direction. And, without prayer, the Bible has no real dynamic. Like ham and eggs, corn beef and cabbage, steak and potatoes, the Bible and prayer go hand in hand.

In the Sermon on the Mount, the Lord outlines the three levels of prayer that should characterize the prayer life of each and every believer. In His words, we are to "ask… seek…knock." Effective prayer is wrapped up with His will for our lives. If we know His will in a matter we "ask." If we do not know His will, we are to "seek." If we know His will but the answer has not come, we are to "knock" until the door opens. Many believers never rise above the first level of prayer to the level of seeking much less knocking. Effective prayers are those which beseech the Throne of Grace on all three levels.

THE LEVEL OF PRESENTING A PETITION
("Ask, and it will be given to you…")

We must ask. Ironically, as simple as this may seem, some find it difficult. There are those who are too proud or too self-sufficient to ever ask anyone for anything. Thus, for them, asking God is something that is almost unthinkable.

In the language of the New Testament, the verbs, "ask, seek, find," are in their present active imperative form. This simply means that the subject is performing the action, it is ongoing and it is a command not an option. Thus, Christ is saying here we are to keep on asking, keep on seeking, and keep on knocking.

On this first level of prayer, the intercessor "asks" and has the promise of God that he will "receive." When you know God's will in a matter, you can ask and have the confidence that you will receive. This is why when one prays to receive Christ, confident that it is the Lord's will "that none should perish," he receives the gift of eternal life. However, there are times when we have asked for certain things and did not receive them because they were contrary to His will for us. Quite honestly, in retrospect across the years, I am thankful God did not give me all the things for which I sometimes selfishly asked of Him.

THE LEVEL OF PRESSING A PETITION
("...seek, and you will find...")

There is a higher level of prayer than that of simply presenting your petition before Him, and that is the level of pressing your petition. This is the prayer we pray when we do not know the will of God in a matter and we seek until we find it. This is a deeper and more spiritual level of prayer because it is motivated by a deep desire to want to know the will of God in a matter. It involves an intense search for the heart of God coupled with a regular pattern of Bible reading. It is at this point that the Apostle Paul admonishes us to "let the Word of Christ dwell in you richly in all wisdom" (Colossians 3:16).

We are to keep on seeking with an intensity that goes far beyond the level of simply presenting our petitions. And, the promise is that we will find God's perfect will for our lives if we don't give up. He does not want to veil His will from us but desires that we know it and walk in it.

THE LEVEL OF PERSISTING A PETITION
("knock, and it will be opened to you.")

When we reach this higher level of prayer, God finds out who is really serious and who is not. To keep on knocking requires tremendous perseverance (see Luke 11:5-8). We pray on this level of persisting a petition when we feel certain we know the will of God in a matter but have not seen it come through to fruition as yet. We keep on asking… keep on seeking…keep on knocking and hold to the promise that "it will be opened to you."

There is a sense in which God deals with us as we do our own children. When they are small we teach them to "ask" for certain things. Later we teach them to "seek" for their desires. And, because we know what is best for them, we lead them to show real earnestness until doors are opened for them. We would do our children a great injustice if we treated them when they were 10 years old like we did when they were 2 or if we treated them when they were 18 as we did when they were 10. When our children are small we teach them to ask for things. When they get older and progress in school, we teach them to seek for answers to their homework. And, by the time they get to be young adults, they had best know how to knock.

We pray on this higher level of prayer when we know the will of God in a matter and, yet, the door remains closed. We keep on knocking. We never give up because we hold to God's promise, "It will be opened to you."

There are times in our Christian experience when we ask God in prayer for certain things and it seems he does not answer us. However, He always answers. Sometimes the answer is *direct*, that is, we pray and almost immediately we see the answer. Other times His answer is *denied*. He answers, but in a way in which our request is denied because He knows what is best for us. There are also times when the answer is *delayed*. God seems to put us in a holding pattern and the answer eventually comes on His timetable instead of ours. And, then, there are answers which are *different* than we expected. Just because He answers our prayers in a different manner than we anticipated does not mean they are not answered.

As you memorize this verse this week, meditate on these three different levels of prayer and don't simply ask, but seek. And yes, keep on knocking. Never give up. We have His precious promises, "…It will be given to you…you will find…it will be opened to you."

CHAPTER 9:
The Proof Is in the Pudding

*"And do not be drunk with wine, in which is dissipation,
but be filled with the Spirit" (Ephesians 5:18).*

The secret of the Christian life is not that it is a changed life; but, an exchanged life. It is not that we simply take on a few new sets of moral standards and attempt to change our attitudes and our activities. At the moment of conversion we give God our old life, He puts it away, and He comes to live in us in the person of the Holy Spirit. His promise to us is that He will abide there, never to leave us, filling us and empowering us for service.

Paul makes a contrast here between being "drunk with wine" and being "filled with the Spirit." The former causes one to be out of control, the other enables one to be in control. One is counterproductive, the other is productive. One makes one powerless, the other empowers. One often brings sorrow, the other brings joy.

The admonition of our verse is a mandate, a command, "Be filled with the Spirit." God does not leave this as an option for the believer. Every verb has a number, a tense, a voice and a mood. When this command to "be filled" is broken down, it is of interest to note that the number is plural. The tense is present; that is, continuous action is involved here. The voice is passive which means the subject doesn't act; it is acted upon by some outside force. The mood is imperative. It is a command. Thus, properly translated, the Bible is saying, "All of us must always be being filled with the Holy Spirit."

How can we know that we are being filled with God's Spirit? Better still, how will others know? Some contend it is in the reception and use of certain "gifts of the Spirit." However, Scripture teaches quite the opposite in the very context of this command. As the old adage says, "The proof is in the pudding." The three verses following reveal to us the evidence by which we can know that Ephesians 5:18 is fulfilled in our lives. Yes, the proof is in the pudding.

THERE IS AN INWARD EVIDENCE
("...Singing and making melody in your heart to the Lord." [Ephesians 5:19])

The first evidence that we are being controlled and filled by God's Spirit is that we will have a song in our heart. This is the inward evidence. Buddhists may have their impressive temples, but they have no song in their hearts. Hindus may have their mantras, but there is no song in their hearts. Islam may pride herself in alms-giving and perceived morality, but where is the song?

Notice that the Bible says we are not making "rhythm" in our hearts. Rhythm generally appeals to the flesh. Nor, does it say we are making "harmony" which appeals to the soulish realm of our emotions. It is the "melody" which gives us the song and appeals to the inner Spirit. Like Paul and Silas in a Philippian jail at midnight, we, too, can still have a song in our hearts regardless of our circumstances.

THERE IS AN UPWARD EVIDENCE *("Giving thanks always for all things to God..." [Ephesians 5:20])*

Here is found an attitude of gratitude to God. The one being filled with the Spirit continues in a spirit of giving thanks always and is thankful for all things at the same time. While we have the confidence personally that we are being filled through the inward evidence of a song in our hearts, God sees it in our continual attitude of thanksgiving for all things, the upward evidence.

THERE IS AN OUTWARD EVIDENCE *("Submitting to one another in the fear of God." [Ephesians 5:21])*

There is finally an outward evidence which manifests itself in our relationship with others. This element of submission does not involve any sense of a lack of superiority. It is what the Apostle was driving at when he said we should "esteem others as better than ourselves"(Philippians 2:3). This was never more beautifully illustrated than in the Upper Room when our Lord Himself became the servant of all and washed His disciple's feet. The one who is being controlled by God's Spirit within will have a song in his heart, will be thankful always for all things, and will be submissive in dealings with others.

How can we be filled with the Spirit who lives in us

through the new birth? Step one is to CONFESS. We must come clean with Him. 1 John 1:9 says, "If we confess our sins, he is faithful and just to forgive us our sins and to cleanse us from all unrighteousness." The next step is to CROWN Jesus the Lord of our life. Romans 14:9 says, "To this end Christ both died and rose and lived again, that He might be Lord of both the dead and the living." Finally, we are to CLAIM all of this by faith. Mark 11:24 says, "Therefore I say to you, whatever things you ask when you pray, believe that you receive them, and you will have them." Confess—Crown—Claim! And, "Be filled with the Spirit." Once you are, then the proof will be in the pudding.

As you memorize this verse this week, meditate on how much God longs to reign as Lord on the throne of your heart, to fill you with His own fullness and to empower you to overcome and live a life of blessing. After all, if it is great to get a blessing, it is even better to be a blessing. Confess your sins afresh and anew to Him. Crown Him the Lord of your life. Remove yourself from the throne of your heart and welcome Him there. Then claim it, by faith.

CHAPTER 10:
The Fruit of The Spirit

> *"But the fruit of the Spirit is love, joy, peace,
> longsuffering, kindness, goodness, faithfulness, gentleness,
> self-control" (Galatians 5:22-23).*

In our previous chapter we examined the filling of the Spirit. We now turn our attention to the fruit of the Spirit. Fruit is the delectable product of that which is produced by the inner life of the vine. On the eve of the crucifixion, the Lord Jesus put it thus, "Abide in me, and I in you. As the branch cannot bear fruit of itself, unless it abides in the vine, neither can you, unless you abide in Me" (John 15:4). Earlier, on a Galilean hillside He had said, "By their fruits you will know them" (Matthew 7:20). The fruit we bear as believers is evidence of the His abiding on the throne of our lives.

At first glance, there appears to be a grammatical error in this verse. Note carefully, "The fruit of the Spirit *is* love, joy, peace..." The truth is the fruit of the Spirit is "love." Love, period. The nine fruits described here are a cluster describing the evidence of the life of Christ within us. The fruit is singular here because it is the outcropping of one life within. The fruit represents what we are rather than what we do. Here we are reintroduced to the principle of being before doing. What we do is determined by who, or whose, we really are!

The fruit described in Galatians is a triad; three clusters with three fruits each. They represent a countenance that is obvious, a conduct that is orderly and a character that is obedient.

A COUNTENANCE THAT IS OBVIOUS
("...Love, joy, peace...")

Certain individuals seem to emanate a countenance of love, joy and peace. The word translated "love" here is agape, God's own love. This is the highest level of love which always seeks the other's highest good. It is the same word we found back in John 3:16 when "God so loved the world." It is no coincidence that love is first on the list of nine pieces of fruit here. It is the fountain of all others. Everything good issues out of God's love.

Next, comes joy. It is the inner joy of Christ in the life of the believer that expresses itself through our very countenence. This is the joy spoken of by Christ to His disciples on His last night in their presence, "These things I have spoken to you, that My joy may remain in you, and that your joy may be full" (John 15:11). If ever there was an attribute that is deserving of a place next to love, it is joy.

Peace makes up this triad which is obvious in the countenance of the Spirit-controlled believer. Inner peace is God's very special gift to us. Again, on the evening before His death on the cross, we hear these words escaping His lips, "Peace I leave with you, My peace I give to you; not as the world gives do I give to you. Let not your heart be troubled, neither let it be afraid" (John 14:27). When we are abiding in the Spirit, the natural outcome is love, joy and peace. It becomes obvious in our very countenance.

A CONDUCT THAT IS ORDERLY
("...longsuffering, kindness, goodness...")

Longsuffering is synonymous with patience. This translates a compound word in Greek meaning to be "far from anger." This type of conduct, which is virtually void of a spirit of retaliation, cannot be worked up. It is produced from within. In our fast-paced, self-seeking world, patience does not seem to be in high demand. Like all the others in this cluster of fruit, longsuffering emits from love. Love's greatest triumph is not always in what love does, but, more often than not, it is in what love refrains from doing.

The conduct of one who is abiding in Christ is also characterized by kindness. This same Greek word appears in the Ephesian epistle, "That in the ages to come He might show the exceeding riches of His grace in His kindness toward us in Christ Jesus" (Ephesians 2:7). Since Christ shows His kindness to us and He abides within, we are to pass this kindness on to others with a conduct that is orderly.

Paul now introduces the fruit of goodness. Jesus "went about doing good" (Acts 10:38). There is a genuine sense of "goodness" about those who are abiding in Christ and being controlled by His Spirit. This orderly conduct is seen in the lives of many who have come to Christ. Where once they may have been impatient, now they have supernatural patience. Where once they were self-centered, now they show kindness toward others. Where once they may have been self-seeking, now they are characterized by goodness.

A CHARACTER THAT IS OBEDIENT
("...faithfulness, gentleness, self-control...")

What better could be said of someone than he or she is characterized by faithfulness. Jesus reminds us that, "He who is faithful in what is least, is faithful also in much" (Luke 16:10). When we live a life of faithfulness, there is something inherent about it that strengthens our own self-worth.

Another fruit that issues out of the abiding life in Christ is gentleness. This is the same word we translate "meek" in Matthew 5:5. On the surface it sounds a bit weak. However, it is one of the strongest character traits that can exist. The word picture is of a stallion that has been domesticated. Or, as the cowboys here in Texas would say, "The horse has been broken." Once it was a bucking bronco and now it has a gentleness about it. This Greek word speaks of power on a leash. It describes one who has come under the control of a master. Gentleness is the natural outflow of that one life within.

Finally, we come to the last piece of fruit in our cluster — self-control. It is impossible to achieve the highest level of self-control apart from God's abiding Spirit within us. Self-control does not come by the outworking of mere fleshly energy and effort. Like all the rest of the fruit, it is the outcropping of the life of the Holy Spirit within us. When we come to know Christ as a personal Savior, the Father sends the Holy Spirit not only to seal us, indwell us, and fill us, but to produce fruit through us.

As we memorize this verse this week, meditate on a few questions. What about my countenance? Do others see love, joy and peace in me? What about my conduct? Are patience, kindness and goodness characteristic of who I am? What about my character? Do I exhibit faithfulness, gentleness, and self-control? The fruit of the Spirit is LOVE! Allow Christ's love to reign and rule in you and through you today. Being comes before doing, for what we do is always determined by what we are.

CHAPTER 11:
God's Telephone Number

"Call to Me, and I will answer you, and show you great and mighty things, which you do not know" (Jeremiah 33:3).

In Jeremiah 33:3 we find one of the most amazing promises in the entire Bible. An old friend calls this God's telephone number. The line is never busy. It never goes to voice mail. He always answers. And, He answers in a way that far exceeds our most optimistic expectations.

Prayer is one of the awesome privileges of the Christian life. Jesus said, "My house shall be called a house of prayer" (Mark 11:17). Before it is to be called a house of Bible teaching or the house of evangelism or the house of discipleship or the house of social action, His house is to be called the "house of prayer." It is also of interest to note that the disciples asked of him, "Lord, teach us to pray" (Luke 11:1). They never asked Him to teach them to preach or to evangelize or to organize or mobilize. The only thing recorded that these faithful followers requested was that they be taught to pray. They observed Him for three years. They saw the intensity and frequency of His own personal prayer life. They knew that if they could capture the essence of prayer, they would be well on their way to preaching or any of the other ministries needed to be performed.

As we dial up God's telephone number today, let's join

the disciples in this request, "Lord, teach us to pray."

WHAT IS PRAYER?

Is the art of prayer consumed with praying ancient prayers by rote or ritual? God said, "Call to Me." Prayer is two-way communication. It is not just one sided. On the Emmaus Road the two disciples exclaimed, "Did not our heart burn within us while (Jesus) talked with us on the road, and while He opened the Scriptures to us?" (Luke 24:32). Burning hearts come when we hear from Him and we hear from Him as did they, when He opens the Scripture to us.

Prayer is the talking part of a relationship. To have a positive and productive relationship with our wives, husbands, children, parents or whomever else, there must be verbal communication. An early sign that a relationship is going sour is a lack of communication. And yet, some Christians think they can go for days, or even weeks, without communication with God. Prayer is the talking part of our relationship with the Lord and is vital for our own spiritual growth.

WHY PRAY?

We should pray because the Lord knows better than we what we really need. It is prayer that makes God real to us. Just as the Bible gives our prayer direction, it is prayer that brings a new dynamic to our Bible reading. God speaks to us through His Word. We speak to Him through prayer. Prayer is like a symphony. The Bible is the score. The Holy Spirit is the conductor. And, we are the instruments. As we read God's word the Holy Spirit leads us in our prayer life as we actually begin to pray the Scriptures for ourselves and others.

Another reason we should pray is because Jesus prayed. Think about it. If He, who never sinned, saw the need to pray so often, how much more do we, sinful as we are, need to call upon Him? Prayer has a way of setting us free. "The Lord restored Job's losses when he prayed for his friends" (Job 42:10). We should also pray because of the multitude of prayer promises we find in the Scriptures, not the least of which is Jeremiah 33:3.

WHEN TO PRAY?

The Bible encourages us to "pray without ceasing" (1 Thessalonians 2:13). That is, we should live our lives in a constant state of communion with Him as we go about our work and witness. Our Lord prayed "a long while before daylight" (Mark 1:35). On occasion, He spent whole nights in prayer (Luke 6:12). He prayed before each great crisis of life as evidenced of His prayer at the tomb of Lazarus. He prayed after the great accomplishments of life as evidenced after He fed the multitudes on the Galilean hillside. Gethsemane reminds us of how He prayed before the great temptations of life. The busier our Lord's life became, the more He gave priority to His own prayer life.

HOW TO PRAY?

The place to begin in prayer is with the prayer of confession (Isaiah 59:1-2; Psalm 66:18). There is a sense in which it is not so much what we pray as it is what we are when we pray. To confess means to agree with God. Our sin is not something to be minimized because it may not be as bad as someone else's. Nor, is it to be excused because everyone else is doing it. Nor, is it some little vice to be laughed off. Sin is so serious it necessitated the cross. In this initial part of our prayer experience, we should confess sins of the tongue, things we may have said. We should confess sins of action, things we may have done. We should confess sins of thought, those things we have allowed to reside in our minds. We should also confess sins of omission, for to know to do right and not to do it is also sin according to the Bible. We have the promise that "if we confess our sins, He is faithful and just to forgive us our sins and to cleanse us from all unrighteousness" (1 John 1:9).

Next, we progress in our prayer to the prayer of thanksgiving. We are to "Enter His gates with thanksgiving, and into His courts with praise" (Psalm 100:4). Thanksgiving is the gate through which we enter the throne room of prayer. Here we thank God for material blessings, physical blessings, spiritual blessings, and certain people who are important to us. Thanksgiving has a liberating effect. In fact, it was when Jonah prayed "with the voice of thanksgiving" (Jonah 2:9) that the Lord delivered him from the belly of the fish.

The prayer of confession and the prayer of thanksgiving lead us to the prayer of praise. Now that we have entered the gate of thanksgiving we step into "the courts with praise" (Psalm 100:4). We thank God for what He has done; we praise Him for who He is! In the prayer of praise we remember the question of our Lord to Peter, "Do you love me more than these?" (John 21:15). Here we tell Him we love Him. We praise Him for His great attributes; His goodness, patience, holiness, mercy and the like. It is helpful to repeat stanzas of praise hymns to Him at this level of prayer.

This brings us next to the prayer of intercession. Here we approach His throne in behalf of others for whom we are praying. This is the prayer for our individual family members, friends, political leaders both national and local, those who need Christ, and even those who may have spoken against us.

After the prayer of intercession, we move to the prayer of petition. Here we ask God for anything and everything He may have put on our heart. Finally, we arrive at the prayer of communion. This is the prayer which goes beyond mere words, when, with an open Bible, we are still and "listen to God." When I first dated my wife, we talked incessantly, both afraid the other might think we were boring if the conversation lulled. However, after a few months, we would sit on her parents' sofa for long periods without saying a word...but we were communicating! And so it is with the prayer of communion. This is the prayer that goes beyond mere words.

As you memorize God's telephone number, meditate on the reality that prayer is a vital part of Scripture memory and meditation. The Bible and prayer are inseparable. Call to Him…He will answer you…and, He will show you (He will let you see it) not just some things, but "great and mighty things which you do not know."

CHAPTER 12:
Did The Devil Really Make Me Do It?

"No temptation has overtaken you except such as is common to man; but God is faithful, who will not allow you to be tempted beyond what you are able, but with the temptation will also make the way of escape, that you may be able to bear it" (1 Corinthians 10:13).

Early on in my Christian pilgrimage I discovered the value of Scripture memory. This verse, 1 Corinthians 10:13, was the first verse I ever deposited in the memory bank of my mind. Because I had hid this verse in my heart, only God has recorded how many times across the years when I found myself faced with some sort of temptation, it surfaced in my memory and kept me from many a potential mistake. Scripture memory plays a vital role in overcoming temptation. D. L. Moody's worn Bible, from which he preached to millions in the nineteenth century, had these words written in his own hand in the fly-leaf, "Sin will keep you from the Bible — or — the Bible will keep you from sin."

It is not a sin to be tempted. Temptation comes our way in all sorts of forms and sizes. Our minds are like a hotel. The manager cannot keep someone from entering the lobby. However, he can certainly keep him from getting a room. It is not a sin when a temptation passes through our mind.

The sin comes when it does not do that; when it doesn't pass through our mind. The sin comes when we give that thought a room in our mind and let it dwell there.

One should not confuse temptations with trials that may come our way. Most often, trials are allowed, or even sent, by God to cause the Christian to stand. Temptations are sent from the devil to cause the Christian to stumble. "Let no one say when he is tempted, 'I am tempted by God', for God cannot be tempted by evil, nor does He Himself tempt anyone. But each one is tempted when he is drawn away by his own desires and enticed" (James 1:13-14). The devil never made us do anything. He simply dangles the bait in from of us. Then we are "tempted when we are drawn away by our own desires and enticed" by that which is outside the boundaries laid out for us in God's Word.

THE REALITY OF TEMPTATION
("No temptation has overtaken you except such as is common to man...")

Make no mistake about it. We will be tempted. As long as we are encased in human flesh, it desires to rebel against what is good and godly. We never have to teach our children to disobey. They pick right up on it. We have to teach them to obey. So it is with us and the issue of temptation. It is a reality that is not going away. Consequently, it behooves us to know how to deal with it when it comes.

Some live with the erroneous conception that the longer we walk the Christian path and the deeper we go with God, the less we will be tempted. None of us will ever arrive at the place when temptation will not be looming before us in some form or fashion. Most of the great heroes of the Bible faced their greatest temptations near the end of their pilgrimage rather than in the beginning. This was certainly true of Moses, Elijah and David.

There is a word of assurance here for those who may feel a sort of pseudo guilt over being tempted. It is a reality. "No temptation has overtaken you except such as is common to man." It is inevitable. Temptation is "common to man."

THE REMINDER IN TEMPTATION
("...But God is faithful...")

Life may have its shadows but one thing is certain; they are never caused by His turning or by His changing. He is faithful. James reminds us that, "Every good gift and every perfect gift is from above, and comes down from the Father of lights, with whom there is no variation or shadow or turning" (James 1:17).

Years ago while in the process of memorizing James 1:17 above, I found myself one night in a parking lot standing under a light. When I stood directly under it, no shadow was cast. However, as I stepped away from the light, I began to see my shadow in front of me. The farther I walked, the larger the shadow, until finally when walking far enough I was in the darkness. The shadow was caused by my turning, my changing, and not by the light. Difficulties in life are never caused by His turning or changing. We can rest in the reality that even though we may be tempted, we have a Lord who is faithful.

THE REMEDY OF TEMPTATION

("…He will not allow you to be tempted beyond what you are able, but with the temptation will also make the way of escape…")

God has a way of "escape" for us. The word picture here is of a mountain pass. The idea is of an army that is apparently surrounded, and then suddenly they see an escape route to safety through a mountain pass. No one needs to succumb to the temptations which come our way. Jesus will make a way of "escape." Many who have fallen into sin did so willfully because they refused to take the path of escape which the Lord put before them.

You say, "I am tempted." The Lord says, "What else is new? I, too, was tempted in all points as you, yet without sin" (Hebrews 4:15). He taught us how to overcome our temptation. For forty days He was tempted of the devil in the wilderness of Judea. On each occurrence He overcame by quoting Scripture. The Word, hidden in our hearts, will keep us from sin when applied by faith to our lives.

We should not be surprised when temptation comes our way. It is, after all, "common to man." But Christ Himself is our way of escape. And, one thing can certainly be said of Him — "He is faithful."

As you memorize this verse this week, meditate on the words of James, "Blessed is the man who endures temptation; for when he has been approved, he will receive the crown of life which the Lord has promised to those who love Him" (James 1:12).

CHAPTER 13:
Understanding Our Salvation

> *"Being confident of this very thing, that He who has begun a good work in you will complete it until the day of Jesus Christ" (Philippians 1:6).*

Many personal salvation testimonies go something like this — "I heard the gospel of Jesus Christ...I decided to open my life to Him...I came to Jesus...I gave Him my heart...I received Him...I repented of my sins...I decided to follow Jesus." Note the continual use of the perpendicular pronoun as if it all depended upon me. When we get to heaven, we will find out how little we actually had to do with it all and how much the reality of our verse today is true—"He who has begun a good work in you." Salvation is from start to finish, from first to last, the work of God, Himself, in us. He sought us. He found us. He began the good work in us. He keeps us. And, one day, He will present us faultless before His Father's throne. After all, it was the shepherd himself who went after the sheep until he found it, then carried it on his shoulders safely back to the fold rejoicing all the while (Luke 15:1-7).

THE ORIGIN OF OUR SALVATION *("...He who has begun a good work in you...")*

Who began the good work in you? The Lord. You reply,

"I thought I did. I thought I repented. I thought I came to Christ. I thought I took the initiative." No, God did. Just as in the early chapters of Genesis He took the skins of an innocent, sacrificial animal to cover the sin of Adam and Eve, so God is still the initiator in covering our sins today. Fig leaves will not do. Solomon was on target when he said, "He who covers his sins will not prosper, but whoever confesses and forsakes them will have mercy" (Proverbs 28:13).

In our natural condition we are unresponsive to the gospel (Romans 5:12). The Bible refers to us as "dead" in our sins. We are also unperceptive (2 Corinthians 4:3-4). The gospel is hid to us and the god of this world has "blinded the minds" of those who do not believe. Without Christ, we are also unteachable (1 Corinthians 2:14). We not only cannot receive the things of God, we consider them foolish and cannot know them because they are only spiritually discerned. Finally, we are unrighteous (Psalm 51:5). We were actually shaped in iniquity and conceived in sin. Yes, we all, like sheep, have gone away of our own accord.

Since being unresponsive, unperceptive, unteachable and unrighteous is our condition in our natural state, something outside of us must intervene to enable us to become responsive to the gospel, perceptive to the things of God, teachable, and righteous before Him. Now, since we are indeed raised out of spiritual death (that is, born again) and since we are unable to perform this work on ourselves, then we must conclude it is God Himself who initiates our salvation. This is exactly what our text implies, "He who has begun a good work in you." God is sovereign. This simply means He does what He pleases and is always pleased with what He does.

The origin of our salvation lies not within us, but with God Himself. He takes the initiative. He convicts of sin. He convinces of righteousness. He calls us out of darkness into His marvelous light. He redeems us for His own. Yes, He begins the good work in us.

THE OUTCOME OF OUR SALVATION *("...He will complete it until the day of Jesus Christ.")*

What is the outcome of this marvelous salvation provided us in Christ? It means we are secure. We are secure in the now life and in the next life as well.

We are secure in the now life. Christ, who began the good work, will finish it. He will not let us go. Since we are not saved by performing good works, we are not kept by performing good works. Paul said, "As you have therefore received Christ Jesus the Lord, so walk in Him." (Colossians 2:6). If faith is good enough to save us, it is good enough to live by, to walk in. If Christ can give us new life, He can keep us. If man takes the initiative in salvation, he must retain the responsibility for the final outcome. If God takes the initiative in salvation, then it is God who retains the responsibility for the final outcome. Or, as Paul says, "He will complete it."

I remember when our first child began to learn to walk. She would reach up her chubby little fingers, grab my index finger, and hang on with all her might. She would take a step or two, let go, and fall to the ground. It didn't take me long to learn an important lesson. I began to reach down and grab hold of her hand myself. Then, when she stumbled, I would be there to hold her up and keep her from falling. In the same way, our salvation is not a matter of our holding on to the bitter end. God reaches down and grabs hold of us with His strong hand. When we stumble, He is there to hold on to us and to keep us from falling. We are secure in the now life.

We are also secure in the next life. The Lord will keep and complete us "until the day of Jesus Christ." The day of Christ suggests that grand and glorious day when He will come again to receive us as His own. On that day the church, the body of Christ, becomes the Bride of Christ. Jesus said, "This is the will of the Father who sent Me, that of all He has given me I should lose nothing, but should raise it up at the last day" (John 6:39). Yes, we can be confident of this fact; that He will keep us "until the day of Jesus Christ." We are living now in the "great until." Until…the day of Jesus Christ. Until then, we can trust Him to know we are secure in the now life and in the next life which is to come.

As you memorize this verse, meditate on the fact that

your salvation is from first to last all of Him who loves you and gave Himself for you. Since He is the origin of it all, we can trust Him with the outcome of it all. Or, as the songwriter, Fanny Crosby, once said, "Blessed assurance, Jesus is mine!"

CHAPTER 14:
The Forgotten Word in our Christian Vocabulary

"From that time Jesus began to preach and to say, 'Repent, for the kingdom of heaven is at hand.'" (Matthew 4:17)

There seems to be a forgotten word in our Christian vocabulary. The word? Repentance! The call to "repent" is strangely silent today. Some think it should be relegated to some tent service in the country. And yet, it was the message of all the prophets. It was the message of John the Baptist as he preached in the wilderness (Matthew 3:1-2). It was the message with which the Lord Jesus commenced His ministry (Matthew 4:17). It was also the message with which He concluded His ministry (Luke 24:46-47). It was the message of the apostles as they preached and later scattered over the known world (Mark 6:12). It was the message which birthed the church at Pentecost (Acts 2:37-38). It was the missionary message of the Apostle Paul (Acts 17:30). And, in the last book of the Bible, it is the message of John the Revelator on Patmos to the churches of Asia (Revelation 2:5). In fact, this call to repent is woven throughout the tapestry of the entire Bible on almost every page.

It is not only one of the forgotten words of our time but one of the most misunderstood. What really is repentance? How is it applied to our lives? These are legitimate questions which deserve a definitive response in a Christian world that in some places is more concerned with being "seeker friendly" than in being biblically literate and legitimate.

A PERSONAL MANDATE COMMANDS IT
("...Repent...")

This call from the lips of our Lord is not offered as an option but as a command. Two important questions are poignant to the subject. What is repentance? Where is repentance?

What is repentance? First, note what it is not. Repentance is not remorse. It is not simply being sorry for our sin. The rich young ruler went away "sorrowful" but he didn't repent. It is not regret. That is, merely wishing that the deed had not happened. Pontius Pilate, who betrayed the Lord, washed his hands in regret over his turning Christ over to the crowds. Repentance is not resolve. It is not like a New Year's resolution where we resolve to take on a new set of moral standards. And, repentance is not reform. That is, turning over a new leaf. Judas Iscariot reformed. He took the 30 pieces of silver, the payment of betrayal, and flung them down the corridors of the Temple. He reformed. But, he did not repent.

Repentance translates a Greek word which literally means to "change one's mind." It is a change of mind which affects a change of will, which, in turn, brings about a change of action. This process is beautifully illustrated in the old and often repeated story of the Prodigal Son in Luke 15. After finding himself broke and broken, the company of a bunch of hogs in a pig pen, he "came to himself" in verse 17. This change of mind brought about a change of volition, a change of will. In the next verse he exclaims, "I *will* arise and go to my father." Once he had changed his mind and changed his will, his actions were sure to follow. Thus, in verse 20 we read, "And he arose and went to his father." Repentance is a change of mind. That is it. And how do we know if we have truly come to a change of mind? Our volition will be changed as well and our actions will follow.

Where is repentance? That is, where is repentance in salvation? Does repentance precede faith? Or, does faith come before repentance? Repentance and faith are both the gifts of God's grace. They are different sides of the same coin. Charles Spurgeon, author of the classic devotional, *Morning and Evening*, says they are "Siamese twins, born at the same time." Repentance and faith are inseparable. Repentance alone will not get you to heaven, but you cannot get there without it. A personal mandate commands it. In the words of Jesus, "Repent, for the kingdom of heaven is at hand."

A POSITIVE MOTIVE COMMENDS IT
("...for the kingdom of heaven is at hand.")

There is a phenomena in America referred to as bumper sticker evangelism. Messages are placed on the bumpers of automobiles signaling the desired message of the driver. I once saw one which read, "Turn or Burn!" However, I wonder if punishment is the primary motivation to call people to repentance. Jesus used a different approach. He said, "Repent—for the kingdom of heaven is at hand." A positive motive commends it. His emphasis is on the goodness of God's grace.

Paul was right on target at this point when he said, "... the goodness of God leads you to repentance" (Romans 2:4). Once, when our daughters were small, we rented a house for a week deep in the Smokey Mountains. The first night in that strange place was "blacker than a hundred midnights down in a cypress swamp," as James Weldon Johnson, the great African American author put it in *God's Trombones*. I was awakened in the night by the cries of our little seven-year-old at the top of the stairs. I bounded up the stairs where I found her disoriented and in the darkness. Taking her by the hand, I led her downstairs into the security of our own bed where she soundly slept the night away. And so, our dear Lord finds us in the dark, often disoriented by the issues of life, takes us by the hand, and, as the Bible says, his goodness "leads us to repentance."

When all is said and done, what difference does it make if we drive a luxury car, eat vitamin enriched foods, wear expensive, designer clothing, sleep on a name-brand mattress, live in a mansion on the water and are buried in a mahogany casket in a cemetery as lovely as a botanical garden...and rise up in judgment to meet a God we do not know? Jesus still calls to us, "Repent, for the kingdom of God is at hand." It is His "goodness" that leads us to repentance. Yes, a positive motive commends it.

As you memorize this verse, meditate on what repentance is not…and then, on what it is. And remember, it is "the goodness of God" that takes you by the hand and "leads you to repentance."

CHAPTER 15:
The Bible: God's Inspired Word

*"All Scripture is given by inspiration of God,
and is profitable for doctrine, for reproof, for correction in
righteousness" (2 Timothy 3:16).*

The call to memorize this verse and the intent of this chapter is not to defend the Bible. We do not have to do this. Charles Spurgeon said, "There is no need to defend a lion when he is being attacked. All we have to do is open the gate and let him out. He will defend himself." The Bible will still be the Book of all books when all the other writings of men throughout the centuries have passed into obscurity.

Let's open the gates and let the Bible speak in its own defense. There are several important things to note.

THE DEFINED EXTENT OF AN INSPIRED BIBLE
("All Scripture…")

The little three letter word, "all," is very inclusive. It means what it says. "All Scripture is given by inspiration of God." The Psalmist said, "The law of the Lord is perfect" (Psalm 19:17). King Solomon said, "Every word of God is pure" (Proverbs 30:5). Some find it popular today to contend that they believe part of the Bible, not necessarily all of it. They say, "The Bible contains the word of God, but is not necessarily *the* word of God." But Scripture defends itself saying, "All Scripture is given by inspiration of God."

While there are different degrees of worth in the Scripture, there are not different degrees of inspiration. One might find more personal worth in reading the Sermon on the Mount in Matthew 5-7 than in reading the genealogy tables in Matthew 1. But one is just as inspired as the other. "All Scripture…is inspired." When Jesus broke forth from the obscurity of the Nazareth carpentry shop to begin his public ministry, he was immediately tempted of the devil. He replied with the Scripture, "It is written, Man shall not live by bread alone, but by every word that proceeds from the mouth of God." The defined extent of an inspired Bible is found in the first two words of our verse for the week …"All Scripture…"

THE DETAILED EVIDENCE OF AN INSPIRED BIBLE *("…given by inspiration of God…")*

The Scripture is "given." It is supernatural. It is given by God. It originates with God, not with man. It is a library of 66 books written over a period more than 1400 years by at least 40 different authors from all walks of life. Some were fishermen, others prophets, kings, shepherds, doctors and rabbis. Yet, it has come together with one theology, one plan of redemption, and one theme running throughout its pages, leaving no explanation for its unique nature outside of God himself. It is "given" by God Himself.

It is given by "inspiration." This phrase literally means

"God breathed." God used men but he did not breathe on them; he breathed out of them His Word. As a skilled musical composer creates a score utilizing the flute, the trumpet, and the other instruments, so God chose His own instruments. Some were as different as flutes and trumpets. Yet, He chose them and breathed out His word to us through them.

Inspiration means the words are God's words and He gave them through man. Peter says, "Holy men of God spoke as they were moved by the Holy Spirit" (2 Peter 1:21). Ironically, the identical Greek word translated here as "moved" appears in the account of Paul's shipwreck recorded in Acts 27. There came a fierce storm and the sailors on board, unable to guide the ship because of the strong winds, simply let the winds take the ship wherever they blew it. Just as the sailors were active on the ship, yet had relinquished control over where it would go, so it was with the Bible writers. In a very real sense, the writings were not their own. God Himself expressed this very point to Jeremiah, "I have put My words in your mouth." (Jeremiah 1:9). The Bible does not originate with men, it originates with God. The writers' personalities and styles are unique to them, but it was God who moved them to write by His Spirit. "All Scripture is given by inspiration of God."

THE DIVINE EFFECT OF AN INSPIRED BIBLE
("...and it profitable for doctrine, reproof, correction and instruction in righteousness.")

It is indeed "profitable"...for these four things. There is a sense in which the Bible is like a road map. First there is doctrine, the way we begin our journey with proper teaching which shows us God's way of salvation and sanctification. But what happens if something causes us to veer off the road? The Bible is then profitable for reproof. It reproves us and shows us our wrong turn. God asks, "Is not My word...like a hammer that breaks the rock into pieces?" (Jeremiah 23:29). However, the Bible does not leave us in our reproof, the Bible next is profitable for correction. It corrects our mistakes and gets us on the road again. Finally, it is profitable for "instruction in righteousness." The Word instructs us how to stay on the road so that we do not get off again.

We see the divine effect of an inspired Bible throughout the writings of Paul in the New Testament. He wrote the letter to the Romans to emphasize the importance of "doctrine." In his letters to the Corinthians, he shows it is profitable for "reproof." In the Galatian epistle his emphasis is on "correction." And, in the Ephesian letter he speaks of the need of "instruction in righteousness."

An effective ministry of God's word will do all four—teach doctrine, reprove sin, correct false paths and instruct in godly living. Balance is the key. Some go to seed on "doctrine" to the virtual exclusion of reproof, correction or instruction. Even though they are doctrinally sound, they are living without power. Others go to seed on reproof. They seem to think it is their God given assignment to reprove everyone else in their sin. Others go to seed on "correction." They seem to think it is their calling to correct everyone else. Still, others get out of balance on "instruction in righteousness" to the exclusion of teaching doctrine and thus they have no direction in life. An effective life is a balanced life.

The desired end of all this is that "the man of God may be complete, thoroughly equipped for every good work" (2 Timothy 2:17).

As you memorize this verse, meditate on the fact that when you view the Bible, you do not judge it. It judges you. It has withstood the test of time and will still be the Book of all books when all the others have passed into obscurity. No wonder the Psalmist said, "Your word I have hidden in my heart, that I might not sin against You" (Psalm 119:11).

CHAPTER 16:
Vision Is Vital

*"Where there is no revelation, the people cast off restraint;
but happy is he who keeps the law." (Proverbs 29:18)*

Vision is vital in the dynamic of Christian living. Those who grew up memorizing the King James Version of the Bible remember this verse translated as, "Where there is no vision the people perish…" According to Strong's Hebrew Lexicon, the word revelation (vision) is "to mentally perceive; to contemplate." The word translated "restraint" or "perish" is translated other places in the Old Testament as "to go back." We see this in Exodus 5:4 when those wandering in the wilderness wanted to "go back" to Egypt. Thus, those who have no vision, no perception of what they could be, seem to have no real direction along the way of their Christian pilgrimage.

Vision is vital. Soon after the completion of Disney World in Orlando, someone asked Michael Vance, the creative director, "Isn't it too bad Walt Disney did not live to see this?" Vance quickly replied, "He did see it and that is precisely why we are here today!" If this is true for secular organizations, how much more is vision vital for those of us who are seeking to be followers of Christ, the greatest visionary who ever lived?

Before every great undertaking, there is someone who

has a vision for the task ahead. The football coach has a game plan before the kickoff, a vision of what he wants his team to accomplish. The army commander, or platoon leader, sees the infantry's strategy, a battle plan, before the fighting ever begins. The artist has a conception in his or her mind before the painting is put on the canvas. What a difference vision makes in life. Too many Christians are just going to meetings, following schedules, simply existing and something is missing. Vision, a perception of what God wants us to be and do, is vital. When a believer discovers God's vision for life, it will do five things.

VISION BRINGS DEFINITION

When we truly capture the vision of what God wants us to be and do, it serves to define our task. Many go so far as to formulate a one-sentence vision statement for their lives. This becomes the lens through which they view their choices and make their decisions. Churches need vision statements. For example, one church has a vision statement that says they are making "a great commitment to the great commandment and the great commission." Thus, they keep their ministries in perspective and filter them through the lens that reminds them that if something does not lend itself to loving God and others and leading men and women to saving faith in Jesus Christ, it does not make their priority list. Vision brings definition. It defines our future decisions.

VISION BRINGS DESIGN

This design is seen in the way vision is accomplished. The birth of a vision is like the birth of a baby. The first step is conception. This takes place when a seed of what God wants us to be is planted in our hearts from the Lord Himself. The next state is gestation. Here we "gestate" the vision, think about it, pray over it for a period of time. After a while those close to us see something is happening; that we are pregnant with a vision. Next is birth, when the vision is born and is out there for all to see. Then, comes the most important step for leaders, the stage of adoption. Here the vision which has not been personally conceived or gestated, much less born, is adopted by others and by all rights it belongs to them. Leaders know the next stage is growth. Growing kids cost money and time and so do growing visions. Next, follows maturity when all we have dreamed and prayed for reaches maturity. Finally, there comes the stage of reproduction, when previous visions are reproduced into others and the dream goes on. Vision brings design to life.

VISION BRINGS DYNAMIC

Not much really happens without a vision. There is no dynamic and no motivation. Nothing was happening in Jerusalem until Nehemiah's vision took on definition and design. Then it brought a new dynamic as he returned to become the rebuilder of the broken walls. Vision is what brings a dynamic and a sense of conquest to our work and witness as believers.

VISION BRINGS DIRECTION

One of the most important things a personal vision can bring is direction to our lives. "Where are you headed?" is a valid question. When a personal vision is prevalent in our lives, bringing a new sense of dynamic, it will also bring a new sense of purpose and a new sense of direction.

VISON BRINGS DEPENDENCE

One of the spiritually beneficial things that vision brings to a life is a new sense of dependence upon the Lord. Visions should be so God-sized that there is no way for them to be accomplished unless God intervenes.

The Lord doesn't see us for what we are now. When he first met Simon Peter, he saw him as a "small pebble." However, he then said he would become a great "rock." It was a poignant play on words. Christ saw the potential that was within Peter. God sees us not so much for what we are now, but for what we could be. If, that is, we receive a vision from Him for the work at hand. Vision brings definition, design, dynamic, direction and dependence. "Where there is no revelation (no vision of what God wants us to be and do) the people cast off restraint (they go back)."

As you memorize this verse this week, meditate on the fact that the birth of a vision does not just happen. It must be "conceived" in the secret place alone with God, then "gestated," prayed over and contemplated upon until it is birthed. "Where there is no vision, the people perish." Develop your own vision of what it is God wants you to be and do. It will begin when it is conceived in the secret place with Him. Then, after a period of spiritual gestation, it will be birthed!

CHAPTER 17:
Is Jesus Still Weeping?

"Jesus wept" (John 11:35).

We now come to the shortest verse in all the Bible. Without question, it is the easiest to memorize. It contains only two words; three syllables. However, behind these two words stands an incredible insight into the heart of our Lord. For those of us who attended Vacation Bible School as children, more than likely this was among the first verses we put to memory — "Jesus wept."

There are two occasions in Scripture that reveal our Lord actually weeping. Ironically, both of them take place on the Mount of Olives opposite Jerusalem. On the eastern slope of the mountain, in the small village of Bethany, we find Him weeping over our sorrows at the grave of Lazarus (John 11:35). On the western slope of the mountain, we find Him on Palm Sunday weeping over our sins (Luke 19:41). One can't help but wonder when we read these words if Jesus is still weeping today. Tears have a language all their own. The tears of our Lord speak volumes to us in this dispensation of grace.

JESUS WEEPS OVER OUR SORROWS…HE IS TOUCHED BY OUR BROKEN HEARTS

The event was the funeral of His close friend, Lazarus. With poignant brevity, John simply states, "Jesus wept." He did not weep because Lazarus was dead. He knew that in a moment He could restore life to him. And, those who know the Bible know this is exactly what he did! He wept when he saw the family crying. Tears touch the heart of our God. Mary's heart was broken. Her brother was dead and it seemed Jesus had arrived too late. She held no hope. She was hurting. She was weeping with deep sobs and wails. She was pouring out her soul to the Lord. When Jesus saw her… He wept with her. This great God is touched by our own hurts and broken hearts.

Tears have a language all their own. They speak much louder than words. They need no interpreter. The Psalmist says that God "keeps our tears in a bottle" (Psalm 56:8). If you need God's attention, try tears. It is OK to cry. We serve a Lord who weeps with us over our sorrows and is touched by our broken hearts.

JESUS WEEPS OVER OUR SINS…HE IS TROUBLED BY OUR BLINDED EYES

Most messages related to the Palm Sunday event have to do with the crowds, the shouts of the hosannas, the parade, the pep rally. But all that was a sham. And our Lord knew it. Within a few short days those same crowds would disappear and their cheers would be turned to jeers. Can you picture Him that day; on the back of a donkey, riding over palm branches to the praise of the people? He was the center of attention. He must have been smiling from ear to ear and waving at the adoring crowds like he was sitting in a convertible on a parade route. But look closer—"Now as He drew near; He saw the city and wept over it" (Luke 19:41). Hear Him through his tears as he says, "If you had known, even you, especially in this your day, the things that make for your peace! But now they are hidden from your eyes"(Luke 19:42).

Those Jerusalem crowds wanted a military general who would ride into town and put down the Roman oppressors. Thus, when they realized they were not getting what they wanted, in less than a week, they crowned Him as a King alright; but with a crown of thorns. They stripped him naked, beat him, and asked, "Are you the King of the Jews?" What a joke, they thought. And they laughed. He was, in fact, a King, but His kingdom was not of this world. His was a kingdom of our hearts. And, so our Lord Jesus sat on the Mount of Olives and wept. Interestingly, a different Greek word is used to describe his weeping on Palm Sunday road than at Bethany. The word here entails a loud sobbing, groaning, cries that could be heart a block away. He poured out His heart over our neglect and sin.

Sadly, those of us in the Western church today do not seem to be weeping over the sins of those around us. We are hardly troubled by blinded eyes. We are watching the decay of a civilization before us. This is America in the 21st century and Jesus is still weeping…but many of us are not.

Many of us have lost our tears. But, tears speak so much louder than words.

The Lord Jesus is still touched by our broken hearts and troubled by our blinded eyes. Is our Lord weeping with you…or, over you today? There is, after all, a huge difference in the two.

The last time tears are mentioned in the Bible is in Revelation 21:4. It reveals a beautiful scene in heaven. God will "wipe away every tear from their eyes." This is our hope. He is preserving all our tears in a bottle and one day He will wipe them all away. King David said it best, "For His anger is but for a moment, His favor is for life; weeping may endure for a night, but joy comes in the morning" (Psalm 30:5).

As you memorize this verse this week, meditate on the fact that we have a Lord who is not far off and removed. He is very near. He is the One who is touched by our broken hearts and weeps with us. And, the One who is troubled by our blinded eyes and weeps over us. These two little words speak volumes — "Jesus wept." It is OK to cry.

CHAPTER 18:
Life's Bottom Line Question

"I am the resurrection and the life. He who believes in Me,
though he may die, he shall live" (John 11:25).

This one statement is among the most bold and definitive acknowledgements of our Lord's deity. The resurrection is what separates our Lord from a thousand other gurus and prophets who have come down the pike. This bold declaration is followed, in the next verse, by life's bottom line question. After declaring Himself to be the resurrection and life; the victor over death, our Lord turns to His hearers, and to us, and asks, "Do you believe this?" (John 11:26).

One of the frustrations of Scripture reading is that, like other writings, it is all linear. Thus, I have often wondered how Jesus inflected this question. Did He ask, "Do YOU believe this?" Or, did he ask, "Do you BELIEVE this?" Or, perhaps, He asked the question thus, "Do you believe THIS?" Think about it. Life's bottom line question is personal, pointed and precise.

IT IS PERSONAL *("Do YOU believe this?")*

Perhaps the Lord put the inflection on the "you" in His question in order to drive home the fact that it is personal. After all, when it comes to saving faith in the finished work of Christ, this is what matters most…not what my mother or my wife or anyone else believes. This is a personal matter between me and my Lord.

In our twenty-first century Gnostic culture, an increasing number of individuals seem to be captivated by various documentaries, movies and books which question the veracity of the gospel account. To many, the account of the resurrection has been relegated to some ancient shelf of obscurity along with other perceived myths and fables. Thus, life's bottom line question is personal. It might well be that Jesus is still asking today, "Do YOU believe this?"

IT IS POINTED *("Do you BELIEVE this?")*

It may be that in asking this question, our Lord put added inflection and emphasis on the word "believe." After all, faith is the acceptable response to the Christian gospel. He was not inquiring of His hearers as to whether they were giving intellectual assent to His claims. He wanted to know if they would trust in Him and take Him at His word by faith. "Do you BELIEVE this?"

It is one thing to know the gospel story intellectually. It is one thing to attempt to conform ourselves to its claims and seek to take on a new set of moral standards which accompany its truths. It is even one thing to argue for it apologetically and reason about it. It is, in fact, possible to conform to its claims without being transformed from within by grace and through faith.

Life's bottom line question is pointed. It begs to know if you have transferred your own trust from human efforts to Christ alone. Has this saving faith, this resurrected life, this "Christ in me" experience, made a difference in your life? Jesus said, "I am the resurrection and the life." "Do you believe this?"

IT IS PRECISE (*"Do you believe THIS?)*

Now, we approach the real heart of the issue. True faith must rest on objective truth. Thus, life's bottom line question is precise at four very specific points related to his claim—"I am the resurrection and the life, He who believes in Me, though he may die, he shall live. And whoever lives and believes in Me shall never die. . . Do you believe THIS?"

Do you believe His claim about DEITY? When Christ used the phrase, "I am," it captured the attention of those around Him. Seven times this "I am" expression is recorded in John's gospel. When our Lord made this exclamation, those around recognized it as an expression of His deity. He was the same God, named "I AM," in Exodus 3 at the burning bush. The most fundamental belief in the Christian faith is that Jesus Christ is God Himself clothed in human flesh. He is not merely some figure out of history or the object of some sentimental story from our childhood. He is God. Do you believe THIS?

Do you believe His claim about DEATH? Jesus says, "… though he may die, he shall live." Many live their lives in total denial of their coming appointment with death. It is a fact…we are going to die! Recently, while looking through some pictures of a decade or so ago, I was stunned. My hair was darker then. My face had fewer wrinkles. It dawned on me that this body of mine has death in it. I am decaying and deteriorating before my very eyes. Oh, I could, like some, have some plastic surgery or perhaps some liposuction. I can eat vitamin enriched foods and try and keep my cholesterol down. But none of that can stop the fact that I continue marching toward an appointment with eternity. Do you believe THIS?

Do you believe His claim about DESTINY? Jesus says, "Though he may die, he shall live." It is strange how so many today live their lives as if this life was all there is. Jesus says that even though death is sure, we are going to live again. The body may die, but not the Spirit; not that part of you that will live as long as God lives and will one day be re-united with a glorified body for the endless ages of eternity. We have an eternal destiny. Do you believe THIS?

Do you believe His claim about DELIVERANCE? Jesus says, "And whoever lives and believes in Me shall never die…"(John 11:26). The Lord makes it perfectly plain here. Eternal salvation is through faith in Him alone and not through human effort or our own good works or intentions. Do you believe THIS?

There are a lot of big questions which come our way in

life. Where will I attend college? Whom shall I marry? What vocation shall I pursue? Where should we live? But, there is only one big question in death. "Do you believe this?" That's it! It is personal. Do YOU believe this? It is pointed. Do you BELIEVE this? And, it is precise. Do you believe THIS?

Finally, note Martha's reply in the next verse— "Yes Lord, I believe that You are the Christ, the Son of God, who is to come into the world" (John 11:27).

As you memorize this verse, meditate on Martha's reply. Would you join her by simply professing to Him, "Yes, Lord, I believe that you are the Christ!" And, then you will begin the great adventure for which you were created in the first place.

CHAPTER 19:
God's Recipe for Revival

> *"If My people who are called by My name will humble themselves, and pray and seek My face, and turn from their wicked ways, then I will hear from heaven, and will forgive their sin and heal their land" (2 Chronicles 7:14).*

This past Christmas season, while passing through our kitchen where my wife was busy preparing the big family meal, my eyes fell on an old note card that had yellowed with the years. Looking closely, I noted my mother's handwriting on it. It was one of her old recipes for one of my favorite dishes. When done precisely as the directions said, it tasted exactly "like my mother used to make."

Within the heart of each of us is a longing for something more, a season of new spiritual refreshing, a personal revival if you please. God has His own recipe for revival in our hearts. He has written it down for all us. "If My people will…then will I hear from heaven…" And, when this recipe is followed precisely and put into practice, it will result in a new spirit reanimating us and enabling us to soar into spiritual regions some of us may have never know.

Much talk of revival is from man's side, man's viewpoint. Thus, it becomes man-centered. For a moment, let's seek to transport ourselves and view personal revival from the throne of God. That is, from God's viewpoint.

GOD'S DESIRE *("If my people…then…")*

God is waiting, willing and longing to send a new spirit of revival to His people. However, He does not overrule our own will. Consequently, there is a very real sense in that while revival is always the sovereign work of Almighty God, it is also conditional. The Bible says, "IF My people…" If certain conditions are complied with, certain results will follow.

God longs to send revival to us. "He is not willing that any perish…" There is a very real sense in which personal revival is not a miracle. It is simply God's promised response to conditions met by His people.

GOD'S DESIGN *("If MY people…")*

Revival is conditional upon God's own people. Hear his invitation, "If MY people…" The real story behind any revival in history begins when God's own people become convicted of neglect and begin to beseech the throne for a fresh wind of His Spirit. Reading the history of many great awakenings reveals that they usually begin with one man or one woman who becomes desperate for what David called, "Fresh oil."

God's problem today is not with the lost but with His own people. Many are pointing to the decay of our culture as being the result of the decline of our moral fabric and the influence of secular, and often downright godless, factors all around us. However, God reveals the real issue is not with "them" but with "us." Or, as Jesus once said, we should not try to get a small splinter out of someone else's eye until we, first, remove the large beam from our own eye. God's design for revival begins with His own people.

GOD'S DEMAND *("...humble themselves, pray, seek My face, and turn from their wicked ways...")*

God's demand begins with a call for His own people to "humble themselves." That is, to recognize and confess their need for "much more." The Christian must be on constant vigil to avoid the temptation of spiritual pride and self-centeredness. True humility involves a broken spirit before the Lord.

Secondly, God calls His people to "pray." The word does not entail the "saying of prayers" but an earnest calling out to Him. Too many Christians' prayer testimonies can be summed up with the first four words of Ephesians 6:12, "For we do not wrestle..." Every true revival in history has been born and cradled in the place of prayer. We read of the early church that "when they had prayed, the place where they were assembled together was shaken; and they were all filled with the Holy Spirit, and they spoke the Word of God with boldness" (Acts 4:31).

Next, God demands that we "seek His face." He said to Jeremiah, "You will seek Me and find Me, when you search for Me with all your heart" (Jeremiah 29:13). If believers today spent as much time seeking "His face" as we do "seeking His hand" we would be on the way to revival. Much of our own praying seems to be consumed with seeking something from His hand in the way of material or physical needs. Perhaps, too little of our praying is consumed with simply seeking His face for personal revival.

God's demand also entails "turning from our wicked ways." Sin that is unconfessed and therefore unforgiven, is the greatest obstacle to revival. As Solomon reminds us, "He who covers his sins will not prosper, but whoever confesses and forsakes them will have mercy" (Proverbs 28:13). Note, it is not enough to simply be sorry for and to confess our sins; we must also "forsake" them.

GOD'S DELIGHT *("...I will hear from heaven, forgive their sin and heal their land.")*

His delight is to forgive and cleanse us of our sin. Why? That we might appropriate all that the cross of Christ entails, so that, as far as we might personally be concerned, His death would not be in vain. God delights more in healing our hearts and our homes than we do ourselves. He is willing, waiting and longing to be faithful due to conditions we are called to meet.

If my daughter and I had a misunderstanding or something that might have broken our fellowship, I would long for restoration. If she came to me in humility, asked for forgiveness and looked lovingly into my face; how do you think I would react? Of course, I would forgive her and welcome her with open arms and an open heart. No wonder the Bible says, "How much more" will our heavenly Father do for us. This great God, who sees a small field sparrow when it falls to earth, cares much more for you.

As you memorize this verse, meditate on the fact that personal revival, while it is God's work, is also conditional. "If My people…then will I hear from heaven." God has a recipe for personal revival. Our part is not that difficult. It simply calls on us to follow the directions.

CHAPTER 20:
Oh, That Sagging Middle!

"I have been crucified with Christ; it is no longer I who live, but Christ lives in me; and the life which I now live in the flesh I live by faith in the Son of God, who loved me and gave Himself for me" (Galatians 2:20).

My father's family came to Texas from Tennessee back in the 1800s. As a boy in the 1950s, each summer we would make our annual trek back to Tennessee to visit my Great Aunt Ann. I loved those long car trips in the days before the Interstate highways. We would stay in her house and I would sleep on an old iron bed with a feather mattress. Anyone who has had a similar experience knows that several times during the night you awaken in a ball in the middle of that soft feather mattress. I once heard Stuart Briscoe refer to the Christian life as a soft mattress. I can relate. That bed was extremely firm on both iron ends; but, oh, that sagging middle.

A lot of Christians live their lives like that old iron bed-stead with the soft feathered mattress. That is, they are firm on both ends. They are firm on the front end; they know that in a point of time they put their trust in Christ and have the assurance that they have been "born again." They are also firm on the other end; they know they are going to heaven when they die. But, oh, that sagging middle! It is the act of beating out the principles of the Christian life on the anvil of personal, daily experience that seems to be sagging.

Galatians 2:20 is the secret to firming up the middle of our walk with Christ. This was the second verse I remember memorizing as a young teenage believer. I knew after my conversion that something grand and glorious had taken place within me. I asked one of my new Christian friends, "What happened to me?" He pointed me to Galatians 2:20. I memorized it that day and have held it close to my heart as one of my life verses throughout the years of my own Christian experience. This is one of the most personal verses in the entire Bible. Like a bunch of bees, it "swarms" with personal pronouns. There are seven pronouns in all, depending upon the English version.

This single verse is perhaps the most complete description of the Christian life to be found in the New Testament. It reveals to us what Christ has done for us.

HE TOOK SOMETHING FROM ME…MY OLD LIFE *("I have been crucified with Christ…")*

When Paul makes this statement, the action is perfect; that is, the action has been completed in the past with continuing results. The mood is passive; that is, the subject is the recipient of the action. Christ did this. After all, we cannot crucify ourselves. We might get a hand nailed or a foot nailed to our cross, but we cannot crucify ourselves. It is also is in the indicative, meaning that it is a simple statement of known fact. The Apostle is going beyond simply saying that Christ was crucified "for" me here. He is saying I was crucified with Christ. It is a statement of fact. He did it, not me. It was done long ago, but it has a continuing effect today.

When Dr. R. G. Lee, the late, great preacher of the gospel, first went on a pilgrimage to Jerusalem he and his tour group came to Golgotha, the place of the crucifixion. Lee, moved with emotion, ran ahead of the crowd. When they caught up with him at that sacred spot, they found him kneeling with tears streaming down his cheeks. "Oh, Dr. Lee, I see you have been here before," remarked one of the group. "No…Yes, Yes I have been here before; almost 2,000 years ago." And, then, the old preacher quoted Galatians 2:20.

As the Lord Jesus hung on Calvary's cross, those in the crowd saw only one man on the center cross. But, God the Father saw not just Christ but you and all others who would put their faith in Him hanging there. When we come to Christ, God takes our old life from us. We are "crucified with Christ." In the first century world, when someone saw someone else carrying a cross, it meant only one thing; he was going to die. We are to take up our cross and live like dead men and women today; dead to our old lives and alive to a new life in Christ.

HE PUT SOMETHING IN ME…MY NEW LIFE
("…it is no longer I who live, but Christ lives in me…")

The new life in Christ is not a reformed life. It is not an improved life. It is not even a changed life. It is an exchanged life. We give God our old lives and He gives us one that is brand new. The Apostle Paul had died to his old self-centered life and awakened to a new life in Christ. While many say, "Not Christ but I," the believer says, "Not I but Christ!"

Think of this awesome thought…"Christ lives in me." If we could literally awaken to this revelation, we would be on the way to "turning our world upside down" like those who went before us in the early church. There is no way to defeat a man who truly believes that Christ is alive and has taken up permanent residency in him.

HE GAVE SOMETHING FOR ME…HIS OWN
LIFE (*"…He loved me and gave Himself for me."*)

These are two realities I wish the whole world could know. He loves you. And, He gave Himself for you. The tense of both of these participles reveal that they are punctilliar; that is, at a point in time His great love took Him to the cross and there He willingly gave Himself for you.

Think of it. "He loved me." We ask Paul how it is that He loved me and he fires back without batting an eye, "He gave Himself for me." He did something about it. He died in my place. His love took my sin so that I could take His righteousness. His love died my death so that I could live His life. He gave Himself for ME! What a Savior.

Perhaps your life is like my Great Aunt Ann's old iron

bed...firm on both ends; but, sagging in the middle. You can firm up the middle by coming to the reality of this one verse and incarnating it into your life.

As you memorize this verse, meditate on the words written by Elizabeth Clephane over 150 years ago in her old song of the faith:

"I take O cross, thy shadow, for my abiding place.

I ask no other sunshine than the sunshine of His face;

Content to let the world go by; to know no gain nor loss,

My sinful self, my only shame, My glory—all the cross."

CHAPTER 21:
Gone Fishing

> *"Follow Me, and I will make you become
> fishers of men" (Mark 1:17).*

"Follow Me." Those were two words spoken so often by our Lord. He came upon a group of fishermen who were engrossed in their lifetime fishing business, looked them squarely in the eyes, and called them to put away their nets and follow Him on a life transforming journey. In Capernaum, he saw a Jew taking up tax money for the Roman oppressors. Again, He spoke those two simple words and Matthew put down his money pouch and followed after Him. Over and over in the gospels we hear this simple call. When we heed His call today and become followers, we then become interested in what He was interested in. Jesus revealed to us that he had "come to seek and to save that which was lost" (Luke 19:10). The truth is, if we are genuinely following, we are also fishing.

It has always been of peculiar interest to me that when it came time to pick "His team," which he would train and then send out with a commission to reach entire nations, He picked rough, calloused handed men who had spent their lives in the fishing business. He did not go to the institutions of higher learning looking for the best and brightest. He did not go to the halls government looking for those with gifted persuasive powers. He did not go to the yeshivas and pick those most knowledgeable in the Torah. He went to the Galilee, to a bunch of ragtag fisherman, and called them to follow Him with the promise that He would make them become "fishers of men." Why? Why fishermen?

My family and I lived on the sea for 15 years among many people who found their livelihood in ways related to fishing. On occasion, I would take a seaplane from Fort Lauderdale to the little Island of Bimini in search of the elusive bonefish of the Bimini flats, pound for pound the greatest sports fish to be found anywhere. My guide was always the legendary "Bonefish Sam" Ellis. He was older then but could still spot a dorsal fin from a football field away. We would fish all day under the blistering island sun. Once, while on my way home, flying back toward the sunset, I wrote down a few words in my journal to describe this seasoned legend of the flats. It dawned on me that what I saw in "Bonefish Sam" is what Jesus is looking for in His followers today. And, it is at the very heart of why He called fishermen to follow Him.

A REAL FISHERMAN IS POSITIVE

As we left the dock, Sam would always exclaim something to the effect, "Today is the Day! There is a world, record bonefish out there just waiting for us to catch him." He was so positive that by the time we got to the fishing location, I was so pumped up I was already thinking about where I would place my mounted world record. This attitude is characteristic of all real fishermen. A real fisherman is always just one cast away from landing the big one.

This is the type of person Jesus calls to follow Him. He is after those who are positive; those who see an answer in every problem, not those who look for problems in every answer. A real fisherman is positive.

A REAL FISHERMAN IS PERSISTENT

"Bonefish Sam" was persistency personified! On a given day, by noon we had been blistered by the sun, battered by the waves, and to top it off had not seen the first bonefish. I was ready to go back to the dock, sit under the cool of a palm tree, and enjoy a good lunch. Not Sam Ellis! Winston Churchill must have learned his famous, "Never give up" speech from Bonefish Sam. We kept at it through the noon hour and into the late afternoon until we landed a big one.

This is exactly the type of person the Lord Jesus knew it would take to transform a world. He goes after those who are not simply positive, but persistent. He calls folks who have a "never give up" attitude, who keep on keeping on, regardless of the circumstances or situations. A real fisherman is persistent.

A REAL FISHERMAN IS PATIENT

On the flight back that night, the word "patient" quickly came to mind. I jotted it down. Sam never got in a hurry. He revealed to me that day that my own impatience would keep me from ever becoming a true fisherman. In his patience, I noted he was willing to try different methods. If one bait was not working, he put on another. He was not locked into one way of always doing his thing. Flexibility was his password, and in the end it paid off handsomely.

Jesus knew when He called those fishermen to follow Him that one of their common characteristics was patience. They could not have spent their lives at this trade without it. He knew that those who followed Him would have to be patient in future times when the situation would appear hopeless. He is still looking for men and women who are not "locked in" to one way of doing things. He desires us to be willing to try different methods as we "fish" for the souls of men. He knew that a real fisherman is patient.

A REAL FISHERMAN IS PASSIONATE

As the little seaplane's tires screeched and bounced down the home runway, I hurriedly wrote down one more word—passionate. Earlier that afternoon, we had fought a large bonefish for almost half an hour. Finally, when it was within ten feet of the boat and a few hours from the taxidermist, it jumped out of the water, spit the hook in our direction, and swam away. Sam had a fisherman's fit. I learned that day that a real fisherman is passionate. He hates to lose one!

This is the type of person Jesus wants on His team. He is still calling passionate people to follow Him. He longs for

His followers, like Bonefish Sam, to always hate to lose one.

I often think of "Bonefish Sam" Ellis when recruiting men and women to become a part of my own team. I want people around me like that crusty, calloused old fishermen of the Bimini flats. Learning from our Lord, I try to look for those who are positive, persistent, patient and passionate.

As you memorize this verse, meditate on the wonder that the Lord Jesus still uses ordinary people, like you and me, to do such extra ordinary things for His glory. Be positive; start looking for an answer in every problem. Be persistent, never give up. Be patient, try some different methods. And, be passionate, always hate to lose one! Jesus said, "Follow Me, and I will make you become fishers of men."

CHAPTER 22:
True Confession

"If we confess our sins, He is faithful and just to forgive us our sins and to cleanse us from all unrighteousness" (1 John 1:9).

In the first epistle which bears his name, John is writing to believers. Thirty times in these five short chapters he uses the word, "know," in order to drive home the reality that we can have assurance of the salvation freely offered to us by the Lord Jesus Christ. This is the same John who once was a carefree Galilean fisherman, who eventually made his way into our Lord's inner circle along with his brother James and Simon Peter. This is the same John who leaned upon the Lord's breast during the last supper in the Upper Room. And, it is the same faithful follower who stood with Mary at the foot of the cross when all the others had "forsaken him and fled."

Now, he drives home to our hearts one of the real secrets of maintaining fellowship with Christ. That is, the forgiveness of sins. The word translated "forgive" in our English versions finds its origin in a Greek word which means "to send away." The same word is used when describing the scapegoat that is "sent away" into the wilderness. It is also the word used in detailing how the fever "left" a certain person after the touch of Jesus. It is God's desire to "send away" our sins from us. He has provided a way, and this is the issue at hand in 1 John 1:9. Here we discover how to get our sins "sent away" so that, as the Psalmist says, they may be separated from us "as far as the east is from the west" and remembered no more (Psalm 103:12).

FORGIVENESS IS CONDITIONAL
("If we confess our sins…")

Many of God's promises are conditional on certain requirements to be made by His children. In this devotional we have already seen this truth in 2 Chronicles 7:14, "If my people…then I will hear from heaven…" The forgiveness expressed in 1 John 1:9 all hinges upon the "Big If" — "If we confess our sins." Thus, we are immediately confronted with the reality that the forgiveness of our sins is conditional upon the confession of our sins.

The word "confession" is a compound word in the language of the New Testament. It comes from a word meaning "to say" and another meaning "the same as." Confession literally means that "we say the same as God" about our sin. We agree with Him regarding it. It is not some little vice that we can laugh off. It is not something we can excuse by saying everyone is doing it. It is not some sort of mistake which we can minimize by trying to convince ourselves that it is not as bad as the ones many others commit. It is so serious that it necessitated the cross. Often, our own guilt is God's way of saying, "You have sinned." Confession, then, is our way of saying, "I agree with you God. I have sinned."

FORGIVENESS IS CONFESSIONAL
("...confess...")

As we have seen above, confession is agreeing with God about our sin. We say, "Oh, that is not worry; it is simply concern." We say, "That is not anger, it is righteous indignation." We say, "It is not lust, just an appealing glance." But confession does not say this. Confession agrees with God about our sin. What we may camouflage as concern, God calls the sin of worry. What we may refer to as righteous indignation, God, who knows our hearts, calls it the sin of anger. What we may try to say is just an admiring glance; God calls the sin of lust in our heart. Confession gets open and honest with God and there is no forgiveness without it.

Anyone who has raised children in the home has had the occasion of a spilled glass of milk at the breakfast table. Think about it. The glass tumbles over. The mother exclaims, "What happened?" Everyone scrambles to stand up and starts mopping the table with the napkins...except the guilty one who sheepishly asks, "Yeah, what happened?" And so here we are. We cheat on a business deal and God asks, "What happened?" We reply, "Oh, it was the pressure of the economy." Someone gets into an illicit affair and God asks, "What happened?" We reply, "It was simply one of those inevitable things that just happened." No, confession says, "I knocked over the glass...I cheated someone else...I perpetrated the sin of passion myself…I am to blame…I take responsibility." Confession agrees with God on the matter. It does not say, "If I have sinned." It confesses, "I have sinned." The good news is that Jesus Christ died on the cross bearing our sins in His own body and taking the punishment for them all. Forgiveness is free to all…but, it is conditional and confessional.

FORGIVENESS IS CONTINUAL
("If we confess our sins…")

Note carefully, it is our "sins" that are at issue here and not our "sin" nature. God deals with our "sin" in 1 John 1:7 saying, "But if we walk in the light as He is in the light, we have fellowship with one another, and the blood of Jesus Christ, His Son, cleanses us from all sin." Sin is singular here because it is dealing with our sin nature which Christ dealt with on the cross. There are important distinctions between the root (sin) and the fruit (sins). 1 John 1:9 deals with our sins which are to be continually confessed when we are made aware of them through conviction in our hearts.

Our "sin" was dealt with on Calvary. When we were converted to Christ, we did not have to confess all our "sins." Who of us could remember through all the years a fraction of them? It is our "sin" that is dealt with in our relationship with God which cannot be broken. It is our "sins" which come into play regarding our ongoing fellowship with Him.

When our daughter was young she took piano lessons.

When she would attempt to learn a new piece she would make it through the first staff and invariably about half-way through the second, she would make a mistake. She would start over, much louder, go all the way and make the same mistake at which time she would repeat the whole process again and again. How many times can you listen to "I dropped my dolly in the dirt" without losing your sanity?

I thought about her when writing this chapter. This is the way many of us attempt to live the Christian life. We have tried to start over a thousand times. I don't need a new and louder beginning. I already know the first five bars of the Christian life by heart. I need to keep going, to confess my sins and finish the song. True confession leads to true forgiveness!

As you memorize this verse, meditate on the wonderful way that God has made for us to live a life of freedom from the sins of guilt which shackle so many. He dealt with our "sin" once and for all on the cross. He now deals with our "sins" through continual confession and cleansing. As God may surface issues to your mind during times of devotion and meditation, agree with Him and live in the solid promise that is ours in 1 John 1:9. "He is faithful and just to forgive!"

CHAPTER 23:
The Great Commandment

"You shall love the Lord your God with all your heart, with all your soul, with all your strength, and with all your mind, and your neighbor as yourself" (Luke 10:27).

What is your primary purpose? Everything has a primary purpose. The primary purpose of an automobile is to transport us. I would rather have a Chevrolet that started every time and got me where I needed to be, than a fancy, shiny foreign car that only started on occasion. The primary purpose of a pen is to write. I would rather have a cheap plastic one that wrote well than a fancy German pen that skipped and did not perform well. Our own primary purpose is found in the words of our verse. We are to "love the Lord our God…and our neighbor as our self."

All the commandments of God are pure but only one is called "great." And, it is the one dealing with love for God and our fellow man. This commandment is called great because it includes all the Ten Commandments within one verse. The first four of "The Big Ten" have to do with our relationship with God (Exodus 20:2-11). Thus, Jesus says, "You shall love the Lord your God…" The last six have to do with our relationship with man (Exodus 20:12-17). Thus, our Lord continues, "And, love your neighbor as yourself." The first half of the Great Commandment has to do with our attitude and the last half with our actions. Here again, is the principle of "being coming before doing" which we see woven throughout the fabric of Scripture.

OUR ATTITUDE *("You shall love the Lord your God with all your heart, with all your soul, with all your strength, and with all your mind...")*

The Lord Jesus refers to this as a commandment. It is not an option, nor is it a suggestion. It is important to note that this is directed to those who know Christ in a personal way through the new birth. It is the Lord "YOUR" God to whom He refers. You cannot truly love someone unless you really know them. And, you cannot know someone unless you spend time with them alone. The emphasis here is on loving the One who first loved us and gave Himself for us.

The attitude with which we are to love Him is one in which we hold nothing back. We love Him with all our "heart." Jesus once spoke of those who honored Him with their lips but their "hearts "were far from Him. We are to love Him with our entire "mind." A full heart is no excuse for an empty mind. And, our attitude should reveal a love for Him with all of our "strength and soul." In other words, our entire person is to be given over to Him in love.

OUR ACTIONS *("...and your neighbor as yourself")*

If we truly have an attitude of love toward the Lord, then our actions expressed in our love for others around us will be as natural as water running downhill. This Great

Commandment is given to us in the context of the story Jesus told of the "Good Samaritan." He concluded this story of love for others with an admonition to "go and do likewise." Love is always equated with action. Love is something we do. If our attitude is one that expresses wholehearted love for Christ, then our actions will result in love for those around us.

Jesus said we were to love our neighbors "as we love ourselves." Many who have not found their true identity in Christ have a real issue here. Many have little self respect or self love. This is why this commandment is directed at those who have fallen in love with the Lord Jesus for only those of us who find our self-worth in Him can love on the level He commands.

Keeping things in proper order is vitally important. We are to love God first and foremost. When we do this our actions toward others will issue out of a loving attitude for Him. This is the fallacy of humanism. Humanism tells us just the reverse of what Jesus says in the Great Commandment. This world system tells us the way to love God is to love man first. But Jesus says, "No, the way to truly love your neighbor is to love the Lord supremely."

Years ago when I fell in love with my wife, Susie, we were separated by a couple of hundred miles. I was in school in Fort Worth and she was in school in Austin. I quickly discovered that when two people fall in love they like to be together. They like to be together...alone! They like to write each other letters or send emails. They like to talk daily on the telephone. Do you love God? A good test is to ask yourself these questions. Do I like to be with Him? Do I like to be with Him...alone? Do I enjoy reading His love letter to me, the Bible? Do I delight in talking to Him in prayer?

Yes, everything has a primary purpose. The real question is; are we fulfilling God's primary purpose in our lives by obeying the greatest of all the commandments?

As you memorize this verse, meditate on the fact that this commandment from the lips of our Lord is so powerful that in this one verse He put all the other Ten Commandments. "Love the Lord...and...love your neighbor as yourself."

CHAPTER 24:
The New Commandment

> *"A new commandment I give to you, that you love*
> *one another; as I have loved you, that you also love*
> *one another" (John 13:24).*

My high school chemistry teacher used to always talk about the "acid test." The acid test is a sure-fire way to identify a substance. The Bible reveals that the acid test of the Christian life is love. Love is not simply a virtue of the Christian life; it is the Christian life. It is the oxygen of the kingdom. There is no life without it. Everything…gifts, prophecy, knowledge, wisdom…will come to an end. But love knows no end. It goes right on through the portal of death and into eternity. Paul says, "If we have not love…it profits nothing."

In the previous chapter we memorized the Great Commandment. Now, on the very evening before the crucifixion, our Lord gives us a "new commandment" that supersedes the others not only in attitude, but in action as well.

A NEW RULE *("A new commandment I give to you, that you love one another; as I have loved you…")*

A casual reading of this text might tempt the reader to pass over two very important words. For one, this is a "commandment." It is not the suggestion or a mere option. It has behind it all the authority of the Godhead. And, it is a "new" commandment. It is one that, as yet, had never been given. Although the language of the New Testament reveals that this commandment is not new in time (God's love has been around forever). It is new in expression. It is fresh; the opposite of worn out.

Until now, the very eve of the crucifixion, the best we could do was to live on the level of the "old commandment." This old commandment is found in Leviticus 19:18 and referenced in the Great Commandment. That is, to love our neighbor as we love "ourselves." This self-love is a love with limits. It is often conditional on such matters as time or conduct, situations or social standing. It can lend itself to selfishness because it speaks of a self love. It can also be changeable and fickle.

But real love is expressed by a new rule. For 33 years Jesus had given us a picture of how real love was to be evidenced. Up until then, the best we could do was to live on the level of the old commandment of self-love. In essence, He is saying, "For over three decades now I have shown you real love…I am about to leave you…but, before I go, a new commandment I am giving you…no longer are you to love one another as you love yourself, but 'as I have loved you.'"

A NATURAL REACTION (*"…as I have loved you, that you love one another."*)

We are totally incapable of this love on our own. The only way this can become a natural reaction for us is to experientially know the love of Christ in our own hearts. This new commandment changes things. No longer are we to love on that self level. Now, we are to love "as He loves us." Once we receive His love we are to release it to others in the same way He loves us. Talk about revolutionary thinking, here it is personified.

In order to love others on this level we must know how He loves us. His love is *unlimited*. Paul said to the Romans that "nothing could separate us from His love." To the Ephesians, he expressed it as the "breadth, length, depth and height" of love. Not only is Christ's love to us unlimited, it is *unconditional*. It is not conditioned upon time or conduct or situations which may be in play. In fact, "God demonstrates His own love toward us, in that while we were still sinners, Christ died for us" (Romans 5:8). His love is also *unselfish*, so much so that it took Him all the way to the cross. And, of course, we should note that His love is also *unchangeable*. As Paul wrote to the Hebrews, He is the same "yesterday, today and forever." Thus, in beating out our love relationships on the anvil of our own personal experience we will love others with a love that is unlimited, unconditional, unselfish and unchangeable. That is, if we love others "as I have loved you."

What is the result of this type of love? The very next

verse is explicit, "By this all will know that you are my disciples, if you have love for one another" (John 13:35). Perhaps, John put it best when he said, "Beloved, let us love one another, for love is of God; and everyone who loves is born of God and knows God. He who does not love does not know God, for God is love!" (1 John 4:7-8). This aged veteran of Christ's love adds, "We know that we have passed from death unto life, because we love the brethren" (1 John 3:14).

Yes, love is the Christian life. It is the oxygen of the kingdom. It is the acid test of our own discipleship. God did not write in the sky, or send a tract, in order to reveal His love toward us. He sent His Son. Love did that. He "demonstrated His love to us..."

As you memorize this verse, meditate on the fact that the Bible reveals a picture of real love to us in everything Jesus said and did. Our challenge is now to obey the "new commandment" by loving others on this higher level of love, "as He loves us."

CHAPTER 25:
Three Verses for Youth…and the Rest of Us!

"Therefore, whether you eat or drink, or whatever you do,
do all to the glory of God" (1 Corinthians 10:31).

Shortly after becoming a follower of Christ at age 17 someone related to me three very important verses for young people to know. I distinctively remember immediately writing them in the flyleaf of my Bible. Over those first months of my Christian walk, only God knows how many times I referred to them, until they were forever buried in the memory bank of my mind.

Over these almost five decades of Christian living, I have owned dozens of Bibles in all sizes, translations, colors and languages. However, they all have one thing in common. Those same three verses are found written in my own hand in the flyleaf of each one of them.

From time to time in our individual life journeys, we all come to "temptation's corner." That is, the place where we are called to make a decision as to which way we should turn. The Tempter is always standing there in the intersection seeking to entice us to make a wrong turn. The three verses which constitute this chapter reveal three very important and, I might add, imperative questions we should ask ourselves as we anticipate which way to turn at one of these inevitable intersections of life. Let's look at them, learn from them and write them in the flyleaf of our own Bibles.

CAN I THANK GOD FOR IT?

In other words, when we find ourselves at our own "temptation corner" we should ask ourselves, "If I go this way, say this thing, or do this deed; when all is said and done, can I thank God for it?" The Bible says, "In everything give thanks for this is the will of God in Christ Jesus for you" (1 Thessalonians 5:18).

We are called upon to give thanks "in everything." If there is some attitude or action on our part for which we could not give God thanks in the aftermath, then it should be avoided at all costs. Interestingly, we are not called upon to thank Him "for" everything but "in" everything.

CAN I DO IT IN JESUS' NAME?

In Paul's letter to those at Colossae, he admonishes them, and us, saying, "And whatever you do in word or deed, do all in the name of the Lord Jesus, giving thanks to God the Father through Him" (Colossians 3:17). We are not only to give thanks in all things, we are to do all things in the name of the Lord Jesus.

Can you imagine what would happen in our experience if we gave serious thought to this issue? It would make a huge difference in what came out of our mouths on occasion. It would make a huge difference in what we did on occasion. It would make a huge difference in what we watched and in what we read. Can I do it in Jesus' name? If we would ask ourselves that question at "temptation's corner" a world of things we say and do might be different. There is one other question and it finds its roots in our verse for this chapter.

CAN I DO IT FOR GOD'S GLORY?

The Bible says, "Therefore, whether you eat or drink, or whatever you do, do all to the glory of God" (1 Corinthians 10:31). The true believer is motivated by a desire to bring God glory in every facet of life. There are many things which are done and said which would not be said or done if this important question were asked more often.

None of us are immune to "temptation's corner." In fact, all of us arrive there every single day in one way or another. Stop. Don't just rush through the intersection or make a hasty wrong turn. Ask yourself three important questions. Can I thank God for it? Can I do it in Jesus' name? Can I do it for God's glory?

As I type this chapter on my computer, I am thanking God for that unknown and forgotten individual so long ago who shared these vital verses with me. Keeping them in my mind and in my thoughts has saved me from many wrong turns which I have been tempted to make along the way. I have found out that they are not just verses for youth…but for all of us.

As you memorize this verse, meditate on the truth of God's word. "In everything give thanks." "Whatever you do…do all in the name of the Lord Jesus." "Whatever you do, do all to the glory of God." And don't forget to ask yourself—Can I thank God for it? Can I do it in Jesus' name? Can I do it for God's glory?

CHAPTER 26:
The Heart of the Matter

> *"For the Lord does not see as man sees;*
> *for man looks at the outward appearance, but the*
> *Lord looks at the heart" (1 Samuel 16:7).*

When Samuel, the prophet, came to Bethlehem to anoint the future king of Israel, he sought out a son of Jesse. The proud father lined up his six strong and strapping, hardened and handsome sons before him. They were the personification of the best the flesh had to offer. However, Samuel was not impressed. He inquired if there was not another son. Indeed there was. He was a "ruddy-faced" shepherd boy named David. He was out tending his father's sheep. The rest is history and Samuel reminds us that "man looks at the outward appearance, but the Lord looks at the heart." The Lord looks where? The heart.

Now, to "the heart of the matter." What is it, exactly, that the Bible refers to when it mentions "the heart?" The word appears over 800 times in the authorized version. Is it that mass of muscle, about the size of a man's fist that is located in front of his vertebral column and in back of his sternum? Is it that organ that beats on average about 72 times a minute, that in the course of a day beats over 100,000 times? And, for the most part without our conscious awareness? Is it that mass of muscle that beats 28 million times in a year and if we reach age seventy will have beaten steadily 2.5 billion times?

One of the helpful principles in understanding biblical truth is what might be called the law of first mention. That is, there is significant insight to be found as to the meaning of a word by studying its first uses in Scripture. In the early chapters of Genesis we see three clues that reveal to us what we really mean when we speak of the heart.

THE HEART IS OUR INTELLECT *("Then the Lord saw that the wickedness of man was great in the earth, and that every intent of the thoughts of his heart was only evil continually.") (Genesis 6:5)*

This is the first mention of the word "heart" in the Bible. Here, it is associated with the thought process, the intellect. When the Bible speaks of the heart, it is not referring to the actual physical organ that pumps blood throughout our circulatory system, but the thoughts that form our being. This is why we read, "As he thinks in his heart, so is he…"(Proverbs 23:7). It is our intellect, the thinking part of our being.

When we read that "the Lord looks upon our heart" we understand that He is watching how we think, whether our thoughts are pure or not. Yes, while man can only observe our outward appearance, the Lord has the capacity to look into our hearts, to know what we really "think."

THE HEART IS OUR EMOTIONS *("…He was grieved in His heart.") (Genesis 6:6)*

The second occurrence of the word "heart" in Scripture reveals that it involves our emotions. When the Lord saw the rebellion of man it "grieved Him in his heart." The heart is the seat of our emotions. It is not simply our intellect but it involves our feelings as well. How many thousands of love songs have been written about "the heart"?

When the Good Samaritan saw the beaten man on the Jericho Road, the Bible reveals that "he had compassion upon him." One translation says, "His heart went out to him."(Luke 10:33). The night before the crucifixion, with His disciples in Gethsemane's garden, the Lord revealed that "My soul (heart) is exceedingly sorrowful even unto death." (Matthew 26:38). And we have Solomon reminding us that "a merry heart does good like a medicine." (Proverbs 17:22). Compassion, grief, sorrow, happiness are all emotions that emanate from "the heart."

When the Scriptures speak of the heart, they are speaking to us of our intellect and our emotions.

THE HEART IS OUR VOLITION *("...then the Lord said in His heart, I will...") (Genesis 8:21)*

This third appearance of the word, heart, reveals that it is the essence of our own will, our volition. The Lord said "in his heart, I will..." Often we find this volition entwined with "the heart." The Prodigal Son was out in the far country, a long way from home, when his heart was changed. He changed his mind. Or, as the Scripture says, "He came to himself" (Luke 15:17). Once this happened, he changed his volition. He said, "I will arise and go to my father" (Luke 15:20). Then he got up and turned his heart, his intellect-his emotion-his volition, toward home.

It is God Himself, at our conversion, who takes that old heart of ours out and gives us one that is brand new. For He said, "I will give them a heart to know Me, that I am the Lord; and they shall be My people, and I will be their God, for they shall return to Me with their whole heart" (Jeremiah 24:7).

As you memorize this verse, meditate on the truth that while man may look on the outward appearance, God is looking upon our hearts. He is mindful of our thoughts, our emotions and our will. Today is a good time to "return to Him with our whole heart." And, that is the real heart of the matter.

CHAPTER 27:
Finding the Will of God

"Father, if it is Your will, take this cup away from Me;
nevertheless not My will, but Yours, be done" (Luke 22:42).

As the shadows fall upon Gethsemane's garden, we find our Lord so agonizing in prayer that He begins to literally sweat drops of blood. His passion was in accomplishing the Father's will for His life. Earlier, he had pointedly addressed this with His disciples by saying, "I have come down from heaven, not to do my own will, but the will of Him that sent me" (John 6:38). Now, on the evening before He would hang on a Roman cross bearing the weight of the sins of the world, it was this desire that consumed Him. That is, "Not My will, but yours, be done."

God has a purpose and a plan for each of His children. King David rested in the confidence that God would not conceal His will when he declared, "You will show me the path of life. In Your presence is fullness of joy; at your right hand are pleasures forevermore" (Psalm 16:11). The Lord Jesus is more interested in us finding His will for our lives than we are ourselves.

There are issues where finding God's will is plain. For example, Jesus said, "This is the will of Him who sent Me, that everyone who sees the Son and believes in Him may have everlasting life..." (John 6:40). There is no doubt that those who believe in Christ will have everlasting life. This is the explicit will of the Father. But, what about other issues of life, other crossroads which come our way demanding our attention and eventual decisions? How do we go about the business of finding what is really God's will for us, instead of what may simply be a selfish, personal desire? There are some important steps we can take along the way to finding God's will.

BE SURE YOU KNOW THE SAVIOR

It stands to reason that if we are on a pursuit in finding God's will in a certain area, that, first of all, we have come to know Him as our very own personal Savior. Paul made this crystal clear in his first letter to his apprentice, Timothy, "For this is good and acceptable in the sight of God our Savior, who desires all men to be saved and to come to the knowledge of the truth." (1 Timothy 2:3-4).

The initial step in finding God's will is to be sure you know the Savior. Without a saving knowledge of Christ and His abiding life within, one cannot discern the things of God. They are, as Scripture says, "spiritually discerned."

BE SURE YOU KNOW THE SPIRIT

Once we place our trust in Christ, the Holy Spirit comes to take up residency within us, empowering us for service, helping us "bear witness" with the Spirit of God. Paul admonishes us to "not be unwise, but understand what the will of the Lord is, and do not be drunk with wine…but be filled with the Spirit." (Ephesians 5:17-18). When we know Christ as Savior and are being controlled by His Spirit, He becomes our teacher and "leads us into all truth." Being sensitive to the Spirit's leading in our lives is a key factor in discerning God's will for us.

BE SURE YOU KNOW THE SCRIPTURE

In finding God's will, it is essential that we have knowledge of Biblical truth. God will never lead one of His followers to do anything that is contrary to the Scriptures. Paul's challenge to us is, "Let the word of Christ dwell in you richly in all wisdom…" (Colossians 3:16). When we know Christ, when we are being controlled by His Spirit and when we are abiding in His Word, "He will make know unto us the path of life" (Psalm 16:11).

Along with these three supernatural phenomena, there are three practical ways to finding His will. The first word is "desire." God will not call you to a certain endeavor without first planting a desire within your heart to do so (Psalm 37:4). For the one who is abiding in the Spirit and in the Scripture, the desires of the heart are implanted by God Himself. "He gives" the desires that are in our hearts. The second operative word is "opportunity." Just because we have a desire does not necessarily mean it is God's will. If it is God's will, the desire will be accompanied by an opportunity. Next, we are to "keep walking" and trust God that if it is not His will, He will shut the door.

This is exactly what happened on Paul's second missionary journey. He had a desire and opportunity to go to Asia and Bithynia. But on each occasion, God shut the door, "the Spirit did not permit him" to go in (Acts 16:7). There was no rebuke. It was simply not God's will for the moment. Immediately after this, he heard the "Macedonian Call" and went straight there in the middle of the will of God. The Bible says, "After he had seen the vision, immediately we sought to go to Macedonia, concluding that the Lord had called us." (Acts 16:10). The word "concluding" means that it all came together. He sought and found the will of God and the great revival at Philippi broke out as a result.

God does not want to veil His will from you. He is more desirous of you finding it and walking in it than you are yourself. Yes, He has a wonderful plan for your life and He longs to make His will known to you.

As you memorize this verse, meditate on what knowing Christ means to you personally. Recall the day when you placed your trust in Him and were born again. Mediate on what knowing the Spirit means as you yield to Him. And, meditate on the Scriptures for here we find His will so often written for us in black and white. Finally, join Jesus in praying, "Not my will…but yours be done."

CHAPTER 28:
God's Answer to Cultural Chaos

"In Him we have redemption through His blood, the forgiveness of sins, according to the riches of His grace" (Ephesians 1:7).

Our western culture has seen a systematic and degenerative decline in traditional values over the past many decades. By and large, the American church has awakened to the reality that there are at least two generations that have been lost to the church. Culture warriors and purveyors of social trends have identified several common characteristics of these "lost generations."

Among the most prominent of these characteristics are five specific ones which rise to the surface. The number one quest of these individuals is a search for a meaningful relationship in life. Many have never known one. For the most part, they are the product of a culture of massive divorce and they are crying out for a meaningful relationship. Secondly, they desire immediate gratification. "Give it to me now," is their cry. They have grown up in a world where everything is "instant," especially with information on the internet. Thus, they do not want to wait for anything. Next, they want something for nothing. They have an entitlement mentality on both ends of the economic spectrum. On one end, certain government entitlement programs have reinforced this compulsion. On the other end, wealthy parents have given them every material need or want imaginable and they have never had to work for anything. Fourthly, they want guilt-free living. At night, when they turn the light off, they still have a conscience that longs for some moment to be lived over again. Finally, they are on a search for prosperity, they simply have little hope of obtaining it. They will be the first generation in American history, that on the whole, will not raise their children in homes as nice as the ones in which they were raised.

Who has the answers that meet the needs and desires of these future generations? Ironically, the church is the only one who holds the answers to all five needs of these "lost generations." And, all five are found in one single verse of Scripture, Ephesians 1:7.

THE LORD OFFERS SOMETHING PERSONAL
("IN HIM...")

These young adults are on a quest for a meaningful relationship in life. Note the first two words of Ephesians 1:7, "In Him." What Christ has to offer is not about religion or ritual. It is about a relationship, a vibrant, personal relationship with Him. It is "in Him." The very thing for which they are searching is only found in Christ. The bottom line is, we will never be properly related to others until we are properly related to ourselves. And, we will never be properly related to ourselves until we discover how valuable we are to Christ and come into a personal relationship with Him. Christ is the only one who has the answer for the very thing which drives their search for significance—a meaningful relationship in life.

THE LORD OFFERS SOMETHING PRESENT
("...we have redemption...")

The second characteristic is a search for immediate gratification. Note the second phrase in our text, "We have redemption." What Christ has to offer is for right now. This is present active indicative, meaning it is occurring in actual time right now. While they may think all Christ has to offer is for some future life in heaven, the reality is that He makes a difference right now. The day I came to know Him as a 17-year-old young man, I was overwhelmed with the reality that He made an immediate difference in me. "Christ IN ME." Talk about immediate gratification, I found it that day. It is only found in knowing Him.

THE LORD OFFERS SOMETHING PROVIDED
("...through His blood...")

What Christ has to offer is free. It is provided without cost or condition. He is the very thing for which these young adults are searching. And, we are the only ones who have the answer to their hearts' deepest needs. It is not by His power or His love or His teaching...but by His blood that He has purchased a way for us to the Father. It is neither earned nor deserved and cannot be bought. It is provided freely to us through the sacrifice of "His blood."

THE LORD OFFERS SOMETHING PROFITABLE
("...the forgiveness of sins...")

These young people lost to the church are also searching for guilt free living. Again, we are the only ones who hold the answer to their hearts' desires. Only through Christ can we find forgiveness for sins through our confession. Then, as the Psalmist promises, "As far as the east is from the west, so far has He removed our transgressions from us" (Psalm 103:12). Aren't we glad he said the east from the west instead of the north from the south? The north and south have an end. There is a north pole and a south pole. However, the east and west know no end, they simply keep going. He removes our sin from us forever.

THE LORD OFFERS SOMETHING PURPOSEFUL
("...according to the riches of His grace.")

Here we find the real answer to the quest for prosperity. There are more than a dozen prepositions in Greek. Here Christ does not say, "out of" His riches; but, "according to" His riches. If I were to give you a dollar, I would be giving you "out of" my riches. But, if I were to hand you a blank check with my signature affixed for you to use as you will, I would be giving you "according to" my riches. God offers us "according to His riches." God is rich in His grace and mercy toward us. Yes, "for you know the grace of our Lord Jesus Christ, that though He was rich, for your sakes He became poor, that you through His poverty might become rich" (2 Corinthians 8:9).

What are we saying in this chapter? The "something" people think they need is really "Someone." And, His sweet name is the Lord Jesus. He holds the answer to every need of every heart. It is "in Him" and "in Him" alone.

As you memorize this verse, meditate on each of these five phrases and ask God to meet the needs of your own heart at the very points of your own personal needs. After all, "In Him...we have redemption...through His blood...the forgiveness of sins...according to the riches of His grace."

CHAPTER 29:
Jesus: The Only Way?

"I am the way, the truth, and the life. No one comes to the Father except through Me" (John 14:6).

This is the most exclusive statement to ever escape the lips of our Lord. He emphatically declares that He is the one and only way to eternal life, the door through which we all must enter. Without Him there is no way, there is no ultimate truth, and there is no real life. And, if that declaration was not enough, he goes on to say that there is no way to get to the Father unless we come through Him. In a world where pluralistic persuasions are running rampant, it begs the question today, is Jesus Christ really THE only way, or is He simply one of many ways to life eternal?

It has been noted by others in the past that leaders are often characterized by certain punctuation marks. Some think leaders should be characterized by the period. That is, the command, the imperative. "Go here or go there, do this or do that." Some seem to think a leader is one who just issues commands and barks orders. Others assume that leaders should be characterized by the exclamation mark. Enthusiasm! Expectancy! Optimism! In other words, this is the ability to motivate a crowd and instill an air of excitement among the followers. But more often than not, true leaders are characterized by the question mark; as someone has said, "That symbol that is bent in humility."

The Lord was always asking questions. In fact, the gospels record more than 150 questions which escaped His own lips. One day at Caesarea Philippi He got to the heart of His exclusive claim by asking His followers two very pertinent and penetrating questions.

THE QUESTION OF PUBLIC CONSENSUS

Jesus asked, "Who do men say that I, the Son of Man, am?" (Matthew 16:13). This is the question of public consensus. In other words, what does the polling data indicate? Many people refrain from leading and decision making until they get the pulse of what the people want, not necessarily what they need. The disciples had just come from several days in the Galilee where huge crowds had thronged to the shoreline and the mountainsides to see and hear the Lord Jesus. They had been immersed in the Galilean crowds. They had their own polling data. And thus, Jesus inquired about the consensus of the people as to who He really was.

Many today never seem to be able to get out of this verse. They simply live in a world that is much more interested in what "men say" than in what God says. When our Lord asked this question, He was probing, seeking to open their eyes. The answers flew back in rapid succession. "Some say you're John the Baptist, others Elijah, still others Jeremiah, and others suggest you are just another one of the many prophets which have come our way." Unfortunately, things haven't changed much. We still live in a world that seems to be far more interested in what men say than in what God says.

THE QUESTION OF PERSONAL CONVICTION

Now, the Lord gets up close and personal. He asks another question, "But who do you say that I am?" (Matthew 16:15). Do you see it? This is the question of personal conviction. "What about you?" "You...and you only...you and you alone...you and no one else... who do YOU say that I am?" This is the question of eternity. It is the question that must be faced by each and everyone of us. Is He who He said He was; the way, the truth, the life? Is He the only way of access to the Father and to eternal life?

God bless Simon Peter. We are often quick to stand in condemnation of his quick temper and his often boastful comments, not to mention his own fateful denial the night the Lord needed him most. But here, he is inspired by the Spirit and, without hesitation, makes his great confession, "You are THE Christ, THE Son of the living God" (Matthew 16:16). What motivated Simon Peter, who made this confession, to later die his own martyr's death by crucifixion upside down? He indicated to his executioners that he was not worthy to be crucified in the same manner as his Master and made the strange request to be executed on the cross upside down. What motivated this? Did he give his life for pluralism, the idea that there are many roads to heaven?

Did he give his life for inclusivism, the idea that everyone is eventually included in the atonement? No, a thousand times, no! He gave his life because he insisted that Christ was the only way to eternal life.

The very nature of truth is narrow. Mathematical truth is narrow. Two plus two equals four, not three or five. That is pretty narrow. Scientific truth is narrow. Water freezes at 32 degrees Fahrenheit, not 34 or 35 degrees. Geographical truth is narrow. I live in Texas and we are bordered with Oklahoma by the Red River not the Sabine River. Historical truth is narrow. John Wilkes Booth shot Abraham Lincoln in the Ford Theatre in Washington D.C. He did not stab him in the back in the Bowery in lower Manhattan. So, why should we be surprised that theological truth is narrow? It is the nature of all truth. Jesus said, "Enter by the narrow gate; for wide is the gate and broad is the way that leads to destruction, and there are many who go in by it. Because narrow is the gate and difficult is the way which leads to life, and there are few who find it." (Matthew 7:13-14). All truth is narrow.

Jesus is the only way to the Father's house. Indeed, He, and He alone, is "the way, the truth and the life." And, "no one comes to the Father's house" unless they come through Him!

As you memorize this verse, meditate on how Christ is the way...how He is the truth...and how He is the life? Don't find yourself being more interested in what men say than in what God says. He is still asking today…" Who do YOU say that I am?"

CHAPTER 30:
Keeping Life in Focus

"Brethren, I do not count myself to have apprehended;
but one thing I do, forgetting those things which are behind
and reaching forward to those things which are ahead,
I press toward the goal for the prize of the upward call of
God in Christ Jesus" (Philippians 3:13-14).

Focus. That single word holds the key for success in so many different endeavors of life. This was at the heart of Paul's own interest when he challenged us to "set our minds on things above" in the Colossian letter. It is at the heart of his message to the Philippians when he says, "This one thing I do."

The powerful Federal Express company, headquartered in Memphis, Tennessee, exploded into worldwide prominence by simply bringing focus to one thing—overnight deliveries. Southwest Airlines is one of the nation's leading air carriers today primarily because of a single focus on low-cost coach travel with on-time performance. And, who could talk about the element of focus without mentioning the Starbucks coffee chain. When all other coffee shops were busy dispensing all types of food services, they simply developed coffee shops with a focus on, of all things, coffee!

Focus is fundamental to spiritual success as well as

business success. Keeping the main the main thing in the midst of a multitude of other things is always a challenge for the follower of the Lord Jesus Christ. One of the key elements to spiritual growth is the ability to obtain, and maintain, focus in the Christian life. Focus will lead us to do four things.

FOCUS WILL PUT OUR PRIORITIES IN ORDER

Paul said, "This one thing I do…" Not ten things, not five things, not even two things. But, "this ONE thing I do." Focus helps us put our priorities in order. First, you define your goal, and then it begins to define you.

FOCUS WILL GIVE US A FORWARD LOOK

Too many of us today spend our time looking around us, or, worse yet, looking behind us most of the time. Focus enables us to begin to see our glass half full instead of half empty. It gives us a forward look. Paul goes on to say that he was "reaching forward to those things which were before" him. Paul's focus led him to possess a wise forgetfulness about the past and enabled him to make sure his reach continued to exceed his grasp.

FOCUS WILL SET US ON THE SECOND MILE

Focus brings a passion to our work that instills within us a desire to do what is required, and then some. Paul said, "I press…" This word carries with it the idea of an intense endeavor; much like an avid hunter who is pursuing his prey. Paul was "pressing" because he had focus; he had "one thing" as a priority in life.

FOCUS ENABLES US TO KNOW WHERE WE ARE GOING

One of the most valuable assets focus will bring to us is the ability to know where we are headed. Paul said he was pressing toward "the goal." This word translates the Greek word, *skopos*, from which we transliterate our English word, "scope." Like the scope on a rifle, focus will enable us to get our goals and priorities "in the crosshairs." It enables us to know where we are going and how we are going to get there. It keeps our priorities in the bulls eye of our target.

Focus is the fountainhead of successful living. It helps us to begin our task with the end in mind. What is your goal in Christian living? What is in "the cross hairs" of your scope? When we begin to focus on Christ alone, we will find that He will put our priorities in order, He will give us a forward look, He will set us on the second mile and He will let us see clearly the end from the beginning.

As you memorize this verse this week, meditate on Christ and Him alone. Put Him "in the crosshairs" and allow that "one thing" you do to be done to glorify His name. Keep your life in focus by keeping Christ in the center of it.

CHAPTER 31:
Approved or Ashamed?

"Be diligent (study) to present yourself approved to God, a worker who does not need to be ashamed, rightly dividing the word of truth" (2 Timothy 2:15).

One of the great temptations of the busy believer is to stop studying the Bible. After all, in experiencing many years of the Christian life, most of us have heard hundreds of sermons, sat through a multitude of Bible classes, listened to endless CDs and tapes, read a library of Christian books and listened continuously to Christian radio. And, this is not to mention the countless internet websites with sermons and Christian information at our fingertips. The modern believer finds himself with so many resources that it becomes easy to evolve into a mode where we spend most of our time reading about the Bible and less and less time actually studying God's word itself, systematically and consistently.

Paul admonishes young Timothy, and us, at this point saying, "Be diligent (i.e., study) to present yourself approved to God, a worker who does not need to be ashamed, rightly dividing the word of truth." In this single verse, there are four important truths to be applied to our own study habits.

THE BELIEVER'S MANDATE

The Authorized Version translates this command to "be diligent" with the word, "study." We are to be diligent, zealous about the task of studying God's word. Since reference is made later in the verse to "rightly dividing the word of truth," Paul is challenging all believers to take very serious their personal study habits. The Bible is a miracle book, one in which study never ends. It is a lifetime endeavor for the true believer. It is our assignment, our mandate from God.

THE BELIEVER'S MOTIVATION

What is it that should motivate the believer to a lifetime of studying the Scriptures? It is so that when he is presented before the Lord Jesus, he might be "approved" by Him. The discipline of study is a stewardship from God and the believer should be motivated by a passionate longing to please the Lord, to hear Him say, "Well done, faithful servant."

THE BELIEVER'S MANNER

What is the manner by which we should go about our task of study? We are to be workers who "need not be ashamed." Study is hard work. Doing word studies is laborious. Getting out our work tools of commentaries, Bible dictionaries and lexicons is labor intensive. We are reminded that we are about the "work of the ministry" as Paul mentioned to the Ephesians. The dedicated believer is to be a "worker" who devotes himself to a wholehearted study of God's Word.

THE BELIEVER'S MESSAGE

All of this is to be done in order that we might "rightly divide the word of truth." We should approach the Bible with a deep reverence, even a fear that we might mishandle or misrepresent the truth. We should take caution against using every paraphrase we might find in order to twist the truth into our own way of thinking about a matter. We are to be about the business of "rightly dividing the word of truth." This is a serious assignment. The believer's message should always be centered in and issue out of His holy Word.

Think about it….we are God's "workers." We will either be "approved" or "ashamed" when we stand before Him. This is our high calling and awesome task; to "be diligent to present ourselves approved to God, workers who need not be ashamed, rightly dividing the word of truth."

As you memorize this verse, lay aside all the resources and other study helps and aids and meditate on the Word alone.

CHAPTER 32:
Productive Parenting

"Train up a child in the way he should go, and when he is old he will not depart from it" (Proverbs 22:6).

How many parents have stood upon this verse in the troublesome times of dealing with wayward sons or daughters? There is no promise here that the child will never "sow some wild oats." The promise is the child will eventually return home to the truth upon which they were raised. Of course, the operative word in all of this is the very first word of the verse — "train." This promise is not for all of us. It is for those who "train" their children over their formative years through proper conduct, positive correction and personal counsel "in the way he should go."

There is no more poignant example of this verse than in the old and often told story of the Prodigal Son found in Luke 15. The irony of this is that Jesus told the whole story, not about the boy, but about his dad. Here is a father who appears to leave center stage in the drama to his two sons, one in rebellion and the other in self-pity. But, this familiar parable is really about the father. It begins, "A certain man had two sons." He is the subject of the sentence. This famous parable is really the Parable of the Prodigal's Father. Jesus is putting the father on center stage here and not the son. Let's look at him and learn from him.

SEE HIM WITH AN OPEN HAND SAYING,
"I RELEASE YOU" *(Luke 15:11-13)*.

This dad was wise enough to know that the way to keep his child was to open his hand and let him go. Here was a father who was prepared to stand by what he had put in that boy since childhood. Here is the truth of Proverbs 22:6 unfolding before us. Some parents hold on to their children so tight they lose them. This dad was wise enough to know there came a time when he had to open his hand and let his son go. There are always some prodigals who chose to learn life's lessons the hard way.

SEE HIM WITH OPEN ARMS SAYING,
"I RECEIVE YOU" *(Luke 15:20-24)*.

When the boy "came to himself" and headed home, the father saw him "when he was a great way off." He ran to meet him with open arms of welcome. No pointed fingers, no "Where have you been's?" or "How could you have done this to your mother?" — just open arms. The boy came "walking" but the father went "running." We are not talking here about a boy who came home with the same rebellious spirit; simply sorry he had gotten caught. Here was a boy truly repentant. And, here is a faithful father receiving him with open arms.

SEE HIM WITH AN OPEN HEART SAYING,
"I RESTORE YOU" *(Luke 15:25-32)*.

The most notable characteristics of this model father

are his presence and transparency. He was there for his sons no matter what their problems. The most valuable gift he gave them was his presence. When the festivities and home-coming party were at their peak, where was Dad? We find him outside with the wounded, older brother assuring him of his love and support.

We all need to be parents like this one, a father with an open hand, wise enough to know that the way to lose our kids is to hold them too tight and the way to ultimately keep them is to let them go when the time comes. We need to be parents with open arms, always ready to make a way for new beginnings. And, we need to be parents with open hearts, transparent and encouraging.

The real message of Jesus' story is that our Heavenly Father deals with us in the same way. He has open hands towards us. We are not puppets, we are real people. And, the love we can voluntarily return to Him is indescribably valuable to Him. He, too, meets us with open arms. And never were those arms opened as wide as they were on the cross. Finally, He shows us an open heart. He opened it on Calvary for the whole world to see and He invites us into His arms today.

Henry Wadsworth Longfellow said the Parable of the Prodigal Son was the greatest short story ever written, whether in the Bible or outside the Bible. It is, in fact, a vivid portrayal of the deeper Biblical truth, "Train up a child in the way he should go, and when he is old he will not depart from it."

As you memorize this verse, meditate on the loving and forgiving heart of our Lord and ask Him to put a heart like that in you. Open your hands, open your arms, and open your heart this week to those around you.

CHAPTER 33:
The Joshua Principle

"This Book of the Law shall not depart from your mouth,
but you shall meditate in it day and night, that you may
observe to do according to all that is written in it.
For then you will make your way prosperous, and then
you will have good success" (Joshua 1:8).

Success is not a four-letter word! God's will for us, like Joshua, is that we have "good success." Nehemiah, the faithful layman, returned to Jerusalem to lead in the rebuilding of its broken walls with the promise, "The God of heaven will give you success." It is said of Joseph, "The Lord was with Joseph and he became a successful man." And, here in the Joshua Principle, we are told that if we keep the Word of God in our minds and in our mouths, day and night, and put it into practice, we will have "good success." The Lord does not define "success" like many in our world system today. Success, for the believer, can be defined as the ability to find the will of God for your life...and do it!

As the Israelites stood on the banks of the Jordan, after 40 years of wilderness wanderings, God's main emphasis for them was focused like a laser on His Word, this Book of the Law. The Joshua Principle involves three important issues.

THE JOSHUA PRINCIPLE INVOLVES A CONSTANT PRACTICE

The challenge is to meditate on the Word of God both "day and night." It involves a constant practice. This verse is a high-water mark in discipleship. No one before had ever been instructed to receive orders from God through the words of a book. Abraham obeyed "God's voice" when he was called out of Ur of the Chaldees. He did not have a Bible. He did not have a book. Joseph received God's revelation through God-given dreams. Moses heard the voice of God speaking through a burning bush.

Now, as Joshua stood at the portal of the promised land, Moses was dead, However, he had left Joshua the Books of the Law which he had received from God; Genesis, Exodus, Leviticus, Numbers and Deuteronomy. Thus, Joshua was the first man who was to learn the Word of God in the same way as us, from the words of a book. He was to keep it in his mouth and in his mind. The emphasis for Joshua, and for us, is upon making it a constant practice.

We are to "meditate" on it. That is, let it go over and over and over in our minds, to deepen its impression, to set it in our hearts. The word indicates that it is to be like a tune which we cannot get out of our minds. It just keeps permeating our thinking processes. The Joshua Principle involves a constant practice.

THE JOSHUA PRINCIPLE INCITES A COMPLETED PURPOSE

What is the purpose of keeping the Word in our mind and in our mouth? That "you may observe to do according to all that is written in it." By keeping God's word in our minds and speaking it in our mouths we are enabled and empowered to better do what it says, to apply it to our lives.

Reading the Bible gives us knowledge about God. Anyone can do that. Knowledge is simply the accumulation of facts. But, obeying the Bible is what enables us to have a knowledge of God. Many of us obey the Word…partially. We seem to pick and choose on occasion what it is we will obey and what we will ignore. This call is to "do according to ALL that is written" in the Word of God. Our completed purpose, in the eyes of God, is to move us beyond simply reading and studying the Bible to an action of obedience as we put it in to practice in our own experience.

THE JOSHUA PRINCIPLE INVOKES A CONDITIONAL PROMISE

Note the important four-letter word, "then." It is when we obey the Word that "then" we will have "good success." And how do we do this? We do it through the constant practice of meditating on the Word and keeping it in our hearts, letting it permeate our very being and so directing the thought processes of our minds that we speak it with our mouths at points of need. In the initial Psalm, the

Psalmist indicated that his delight was found in the Law of the Lord and "in His law He meditated both day and night." Thus, we then complete the purpose of not simply hearing it but "doing" it as we put it in practice through personal obedience.

Here is true success in life…to stay in the Word of God until we find the will of God so that we can walk in the ways of God. The Word. The Will. The Walk. The Joshua Principle leads us to feed on the Bible because it reveals to us God's will for our lives. And, success is the ability to find the will of God for our life….and act upon it, do it! It was at this very point that Mary, at the wedding feast in Cana, gave us one of the most valuable lessons of life when she said, "Whatever Jesus says to you, do it!" (John 2:5).

As you memorize this verse, meditate on it by reading it enough times to put the inflection on each and every word it contains…then do it. And then? You will have "good success."

CHAPTER 34:
The Second Mile

> *"And whoever compels you to go one mile,*
> *go with him two" (Matthew 5:41).*

The phrase, "Going the second mile," has found its way into our modern vernacular. Its roots are found all the way back in first century Palestine. The Romans had conquered most of the Mediterranean world. One of the marvels of their conquest was a vast system of super highways which they had built to and from their conquered territories. There were more than 50,000 miles of these Roman roads throughout the Empire. At each single mile was a stone marker. These mile markers pointed direction, determined the distance to the next town, and to Rome itself, and warned of dangers which might lie ahead. Hence the common phrase, "All roads lead to Rome."

By Roman law a Roman citizen or soldier could compel a subject from one of the conquered lands to carry his backpack, or load, for him for one mile, but one mile only. As Jesus was preaching His Sermon on the Mount, I have often wondered if He inserted the reference about the second mile when He saw an object lesson unfolding before Him and His hearers. He said, "Whoever compels you to go one mile, go with him two." Can you imagine the bombshell this must have been as it fell upon the ears of those under

Roman occupation who were listening to His sermon? Jesus called upon His hearers to do what was required of them "and then some."

What is it that separates some from others in athletics or education or business or the arts, or in any endeavor? It is the drive to do more than is expected or required. The "second mile" is a secret to success in life. When focusing on the second mile, many forget there are two miles in play here. The first is a mandated mile; the second is a miracle mile.

THERE IS A MANDATED MILE MOTIVATED BY LAW

This first mile is often ignored. In fact, I never remember hearing a sermon or reading an article about the first mile, only the second. The first mile is required of us. The first mile is always the hardest. Ask the distance runner. The second wind never kicks in on the first mile. The truth is, it is not as easy to enjoy things we have to do as it is to enjoy things we want to do.

The Christian life has its own mandated mile which is motivated by the law. It is tough to get started on the first mile. Ask any first-century Jew under Roman rule. The first mile interrupts your schedule when you are compelled to perform it. It causes you to swallow your own pride and bear an extra burden. Often the most difficult part of the Christian life is getting started on the first mile. This is true with most everything in life; exercise programs, dieting and scores of other disciplines. Even Scripture memory! In fact, many try to play leapfrog with Matthew 5:41. That is, they enjoy the little extras of the second mile but do not want the requirements of the first mile.

THERE IS A MIRACLE MILE
MOTIVATED BY LOVE

It is this miracle mile that separates certain individuals from others. The second mile is only made possible by being obedient to the first mile. The second mile has a way of brightening our own road. Think about it. Imagine a first century boy working at his trade. A Roman soldier comes by, calls to him and demands he carry his backpack for one mile down the road. Now, it interrupts the lad's whole day and takes away from his work. But, he has no choice. However, this boy is a second miler. They approach the one-mile marker and instead of putting down the pack, spitting on the ground and marching back home; he volunteers to go an extra mile with the soldier. Along the way, he pleasantly inquires about life in Rome. The soldier is baffled. I have often wondered if that Roman soldier at the cross who said, "Surely, this must be the Son of God," had had such an experience earlier with a second-mile follower of Christ.

One who journeys on the miracle mile also has a way of lightening the load of those around. One cannot travel the second mile without influencing others. It only takes one second miler in a home to change the entire environment. It only takes one second miler on a team or in the office to do the same. This miracle mile, the second mile, is motivated by the love of Christ.

Incidentally, the second mile is the mile our Lord Himself walked. He knows the road very well. It was love that took Him on the miracle mile to the cross. Oh, He journeyed the first mile. He stepped out of heaven and into human flesh. He walked the mandated mile that was motivated by the law. He kept every detail of the law. But, He also went the second mile, motivated by His own love for us. He who made the stars with a spoken word and formed the universe, the One who formed and fashioned us with His own hands, said , "I love you and I will walk with you." But, we went our own way. Then He said, "I will go the second mile." It took Him to the cross where He bore the weight, not of a Roman soldier's backpack, but of our own sin. And somebody told somebody and somebody told somebody else and somebody else told Johnny Keeton and Johnny Keeton told me when I was 17 years of age. I am not all I ought to be today, but I have never been the same since that day.

As you memorize this verse, meditate on what ways you can go the second mile today. It will brighten your road and lighten someone's load.

CHAPTER 35:
A New Beginning

> *"Entreat me not to leave you, or to turn back from
> following after you; for wherever you go, I will go;
> and wherever you lodge, I will lodge; your people shall be
> my people, and your God, my God" (Ruth 1:16).*

God is always the God of newness. The Bible continually refers to the fact that it is never too late for a new beginning. To Isaiah, the Lord says, "Behold, I will do a new thing…" (Isaiah 43:19). To Ezekiel He says, "I will give them one heart and I will put a new spirit within you…" (Ezekiel 11:19). The author of Hebrews spoke of "a new and living way." (Hebrews 10:20). And in the Apocalypse, John says, "And He who sat upon the throne said, Behold I make all things new" (Revelation 21:5).

The words of our text today have become immortal. When famine came to Bethlehem, Naomi, her husband and two sons, fled and settled in Moab. In due time, her sons married Moabite women. The Moabites were a race that was born in incest and observed a false religion that was the antithesis to their Jewish heritage. Later, Naomi's husband died, as did her sons. Left with her two daughters-in-law, Naomi, upon hearing that there was now "bread in Bethlehem," set her face like a flint to return to the will of God for her life. She encouraged the two women to go back to their people and to their gods. One, Orpah, kissed her and went back. The other, Ruth, clung to Naomi saying, "Entreat me not to leave you, or to turn back from following after you, for wherever you go, I will go; and wherever you lodge, I will lodge; your people shall be my people, and your God, my God." These now familiar words constitute the formula for us as new things come when we cling to Christ in such a manner. When personal renewal comes to our own heart it brings several new things.

PERSONAL RENEWAL BRINGS A NEW DETERMINATION

When Ruth said, "Entreat me not to leave you…" she was declaring that even though her sister-in-law, Orpah, had turned back, she, with a new determination, would cling to Naomi. Her mother-in-law had made sure she knew the way would be hard. Back in Bethlehem, Ruth's past and future would be against her. This decision came when all influences were against her; Naomi's insistence, Orpah's example and the religion of her childhood, to name just a few. Yet, Ruth was determined to do the right thing and follow Naomi.

When "new things come" to us they bring a new determination. We say to our Lord what Ruth said to Naomi, "Entreat me not to leave you or to turn back from following after you."

PERSONAL RENEWAL BRINGS A NEW DIRECTION

Ruth continues, "For wherever you go, I will go." In other words, she was saying, "This will be my life's direction." She had never been that way before.

A new direction is always a telltale sign of genuine renewal. We begin to become interested in the things for which Jesus was interested. As Ruth is to Naomi, so shall we be to Christ when personal renewal fills our heart. It brings a new determination and a new direction. Christ becomes the way in which we follow. Yes, He makes all things new as we say to Him, "Wherever you go, I will go."

PERSONAL RENEWAL BRINGS A NEW DEPENDENCE

Next, Ruth declares, "And wherever you lodge, I will lodge." This is to say, Ruth was declaring that she would trust Naomi to meet her basic needs. Ruth had no place to lay her head at night. However, her determination instilled a new dependence upon Naomi.

Ruth would instill this dependence in her children and grandchildren. Later, in Bethlehem, she would meet and marry Boaz, the Lord of the harvest. They would have a son, Obed, who would have a son named, Jesse, who would have a son named David, the shepherd, the psalmist, the king. And David would later say, "I have been young, and now am old; yet I have not seen the righteous forsaken, nor his descendants begging bread" (Psalm 37:25). Obviously, Ruth instilled this dependence in her children and her children's children.

Ruth knew that "home" was in the middle of God's will. When personal renewal comes it is accompanied by a new dependence of trusting the Lord to meet our basic needs.

PERSONAL RENEWAL BRINGS A NEW DESIRE

"Your people shall be my people" was her next declaration. Following Naomi brought a new desire to take Naomi's people as her own. She was saying in essence, "There will be nothing between us." Ruth realized that if she took the God of the Bible to be her God, she would have to separate herself from the godless crowd of Moab amongst whom she lived. It is impossible to fellowship with God and refuse to fellowship with His people.

I remember well, as a young man, when I began to follow Christ; it did not take me long to learn that if I was going on with Him, I had to go with His people. He changed my desires. To love the Lord is to love His people and find our fellowship among them. Among all the new things He brings is a new desire to say to Him, "Your people shall be my people."

PERSONAL RENEWAL BRINGS A NEW DEVOTION

Now Ruth confesses to Naomi, "Your God shall be my God." She was saying, "I am not only taking your people as my people, but your God as my God." If you wish to see an Old Testament conversion it is here. And what a decision it was. Her past was against her. She was raised in a heathen home worshipping false, immoral gods. Her present was against her. Naomi pleaded with her to go back to her own people. Her future was against her. In Bethlehem she would be an exile from all she had ever known.

Ruth was giving up all she knew to follow Naomi's God. Yet, all she knew of this God was a God of suffering and sorrow. But, she knew Naomi and when she watched her repent and set her face as a flint toward the right path, she found not only a new direction and desire, but a new devotion as well. Personal renewal brings a new devotion to our lives.

PERSONAL RENEWAL BRINGS
A NEW DEDICATION

The next verse continues, "Where you die, I will die and there will I be buried" (Ruth 1:17). Ruth was saying not even death will separate us. This decision was for life. Ruth was indicating that this was a life decision. She was not coming back, even if things did not turn out like she thought they should.

We find the same dedication in following Christ. It costs us our life. Ruth would eventually die as we all do. But, she would marry Boaz and today she lives on in history and in heaven as an example for us all.

Most of us know the story well. She goes home with Naomi. She becomes the bride of the wealthy landowner, Boaz. She lives a beautiful existence, totally separated from her old life. The whole course of her life was determined by another! What a wonderful picture of you and me when we truly say to Christ what she said to Naomi, "…Where you go, I will go….where you lodge, I will lodge…your people shall be my people…and your God shall be my God." Yes indeed, He has a way of making "all things new."

As you memorize this verse, meditate on the wonder of how many things Christ has made "new" in you.

CHAPTER 36:
Back to Basics

"But you shall receive power when the
Holy Spirit has come upon you; and you shall be witnesses
to Me in Jerusalem, and in all Judea,
and Samaria, and to the end of the earth" (Acts 1:8).

Once the legendary coach, Vince Lombardi, and his Green Bay Packers, lost a football game which they should have won handily. However, sloppy play and foolish mistakes led to their unanticipated defeat. The next day at practice, Lombardi gathered his team together. He reached into a bag and brought out a football. He then said, "This, gentleman, is a football." It was, in his own indomitable way, a statement that it was time to get back to basics.

As Christ was about to leave his "team" and ascend back into heaven, he left them, and us, with a challenge to be his witnesses not only at home but to the very ends of the earth. A few days earlier, on a mountain in the Galilee, he had left us the Great Commission; "All authority has been given to Me in heaven and on earth, Go therefore and make disciples of all the nations, baptizing them in the name of the Father, and of the Son and of the Holy Spirit, teaching them to observe all things that I have commanded you; and lo, I am with you always, even to the end of the age" (Matthew 28:19-20). His commission to us is explicit. We are to make disciples by leading them to Christ. We are to mark these new disciples through baptism. And, we are to mature them by "teaching them to observe" all those things Christ commanded.

Now, immediately before His ascension back to heaven, He stood on another mountain in Judea. There, He reinforced this Great Commission by calling upon that small group to take His Good news to whole nations, not simply to a few locals. It is a basic tenet of the Christian faith that we are all to be His "witnesses" to a lost and dying world around us. The call to evangelism, to sharing Christ's "good news," is one of the most basic callings of the New Testament. The last words of those who leave us are always intriguing and important. Let's dissect this parting challenge from the lips of our Lord and seek to apply it to our lives.

THE WHO OF EVANGELISM

"But YOU shall…be witnesses to Me…" This challenge to take the gospel to the world is one given to all of us. Two verses earlier the disciples had tried to sidetrack the issue by asking questions regarding when He would return and restore "the kingdom." But, he did not say, "You shall be my chart makers…or date keepers….but my witnesses…all of you!" None of us is immune to this basic element of Christian living; that is, to share the good news.

THE WHAT OF EVANGELISM

You shall receive what? Power! This is the great need of

believers today. We all need power to live the Christian life. Perhaps, the greatest difference in the first-century church and the twenty-first century church is in two words—influence and power. Today we pride ourselves in influence. We seek to influence the decaying culture around us in various ways. But the early church did not have enough influence to keep their leader, Simon Peter, out of prison. They were virtually void of influence with the civil and legal authorities. But, the more important news is, they had enough power to pray him out of prison!

Jesus used a word for power from which we get our word, "dynamite." We need this power to be His witnesses. The book of Acts is the story of a group of men and women just like you and me who went out from a little upper room to tell the story of a publicly executed Jew against all the bigotry and bias of a Roman-ruled world. They did so much with so little. How? They had a dynamite nature about them. They had received "power" from on high.

THE WHEN OF EVANGELISM

When did this power come upon them? "When the Holy Spirit has come upon you." There is no such thing as a Christian without power. When you receive Christ, you have the Holy Spirit. He takes up residency in you. Thus, you have power.

Early in our married life, Susie and I had a new Chevrolet. Well, it was not exactly new, but it was new to us. One morning I went out into our little driveway, got in the car, turned the ignition, and it would not start. Upon raising the hood, I discovered that during the night someone had stolen our car's battery. That beautiful car was rendered useless. It could not transport me anywhere without a battery to energize it. I think of that car when I read this verse. Many church members get all dressed up and ready to go out in terms of witness but never seem to get started. Why? We are in need of a "power" outside of ourselves to energize us.

THE WHY OF EVANGELISM

Note the Holy Spirit enables us to be "witnesses." This is the very reason why we have power—to be His witnesses. There should be no such thing as a Christian who is not a witness. If we are saved, we have Christ. If we have Christ, we have the Holy Spirit. If we have the Holy Spirit, we have power. And, if we have power, we will be His witnesses.

The Lord did not call us to be the judge, sitting in condemnation of others around us. He did not call us to be the prosecuting attorney, pointing our fingers of accusation at others. He did not call us to be the defense attorney, seeking to find loopholes so others could get past the law. He did not call us to be the jury, weighing all sorts of evidence for and against someone else. He called us to simply tell others what we have seen and heard from firsthand experience. That is, to be witnesses of Him. We are not recruiters trying to get people to join our club. We are not to be salesmen trying to persuade others to buy in to our product. We are simply to be His witnesses.

People marvel that God entrusted His holy gospel with such common men and women, void of formal training. They were true witnesses. Incidentally, the word translated "witness" is the same word for which we get our English word, "martyr." These early believers were witnesses (martyrs) in the truest sense. Many of them lost their lives because of their uncompromising witness of Christ.

THE WHERE OF EVANGELISM

Jesus tells us to take His good news across the city, across the country, across the continent, and yes, across the entire cosmos. Here is total participation — all of us are to be witnesses. And, here is total penetration — we are to go "to the end of the earth." The gospel will never find its final destination until it is shared with every person on the planet.

In 30 short years, those early believers fulfilled Acts 1:8. How? They were empowered by the Holy Spirit, and with singleness of purpose, witnessed His saving grace in Jerusalem (Acts 1-8), in Judea and Samaria(Acts 8-12), and to the end of their world (Acts 13-28). They did not play leapfrog with this commission. They did not pass hundreds of witnessing opportunities in their own city in order to go to the "end of the earth." They began at home, in Jerusalem.

Christ's gospel is to penetrate the whole world until every religion is confronted, every error exposed, everyone receives a witness. It is a huge task. But think about those early believers. It seemed geographically impossible. Most still believed the world was flat. It appeared to be physically impossible. They had no air travel, radio, television, printing presses, internet or any of the modern means at their disposal for communicating the gospel. It seemed legally impossible. They were forbidden by the legal authorities to speak in Jesus' name. And, it seemed socially impossible. After all, who would really listen to these scrubby Galileans, so void of culture and class? Yet, they did it. They were witnesses through the power of the Holy Spirit. They did so much with so little and we seem to do so little with so much. The time has come for the modern church to get back to basics. To follow their example and fulfill Acts 1:8 in our lifetime as well.

As you memorize this verse, meditate on the awesome power that is resident with each of us who have placed our faith and trust in Jesus Christ alone. It would do us well to also memorize the Great Commission (Matthew 29:19-20). And, get back to the basics of being His witnesses by "making" disciples, "marking" them by baptism, and "teaching" them to observe all He has commanded.

CHAPTER 37:
Good News and Bad News

"For the wages of sin is death, but the gift of God is eternal life in Christ Jesus our Lord" (Romans 6:23).

Modern culture has been replete with a series of "good news and bad news" jokes. For example, there is the one about the pastor who stood up on Sunday and declared, "The good news is we have enough money here this morning to pay off the church debt and to build our new building." Then he added, "But the bad news is, it is still in your pockets!" Or, there is the one where the church moderator said, "The good news is the deacons have voted to send a get-well card to our ill pastor. However, the bad news is the vote was 31-30!"

When we come to Romans 6:23, one of the most informative and inspirational verses in the Bible, we find some good news and some bad news. The bad news is "the wages of sin is death." But, the good news is "the gift of God is eternal life in Christ Jesus our Lord."

THE BAD NEWS

There is some bad news in this verse. "The wages of sin is death." The Greek word for sin is best understood as "missing the mark." The word picture describes an archer who shoots his arrow at the target and misses the bull's eye.

We all find ourselves here as we have "all sinned and come short of the glory of God." (Romans 3:23). We have all missed the mark and the bad news is that its cost, or wage, is death.

A "wage" is what we get for doing something. We work a certain number of hours and our employer pays us an agreed upon wage. It is something we have earned, something we deserve. It is something we have coming to us. The Bible says, "The wages of sin is death." It is strange how many men and women sin thinking it is going to pay dividends of fun and pleasure. But Satan is a liar. Sin pays its wage alright but its wage is "death" which is separation from all that is good.

The bad news is that sin pays its wage and its wage is death. Payday is coming someday. That is the bad news. When we miss the mark, it costs us greatly.

THE GOOD NEWS

But the good news is, "The gift of God is eternal life through Jesus Christ our Lord." It is a gift, a free gift which cannot be earned nor deserved. We all remember the excitement of opening gifts as children around the Christmas tree. We did not have to pay for those gifts. We did nothing to earn them. We simply opened them and received them. A gift is the opposite of a wage. We earn and deserve our wages. We don't earn or deserve a gift. If we did, it would be a reward and not a gift.

How is this all possible? We still have to deal with the bad news. Jesus made the way possible for us by dealing with the bad news Himself. Two thousand years ago on a Roman cross outside the city walls of Jerusalem, Jesus took the bad news and "became sin for us." Yes, the wages of sin is death and He died our death on the cross, paying the penalty for our sin. He paid the price so we could finish the verse with the good news, "But the gift of God is eternal life through Jesus Christ our Lord." He made a way out of no way. Our part is to receive this God-provided and free gift by faith alone in Him.

What a difference there is in these two bits of news. The bad news is, sin is costly, it has a wage attached to it. The good news is, eternal life is free. It is God's gift to us. And, that is no joke!

As you memorize this verse, meditate on the incredible price that was paid for our sin. When we were so undeserving, He made a way for us to receive the greatest gift ever given, "eternal life through Jesus Christ our Lord."

CHAPTER 38:
Removing the Fear of Death

"Yea, though I walk through the valley of the shadow of death,
I will fear no evil; for you are with me; Your rod and
Your staff, they comfort me" (Psalm 23:4).

Death is the single common denominator of all men. This fact is illustrated every day in the morning newspaper. The business section of the paper highlights only those who are successful in their vocational endeavors. The social section contains pictures and stories only related to the social elite. The sports section is filled with articles about those teams and individuals who excel in their athletic fields. Then, we come to the obituary section. There, listed side by side in alphabetical order are the rich and the poor, the known and the unknown, the prominent and the not so prominent. We are all equal in death. It is our common denominator.

There are a lot of voices and volumes today which tell us how to live. Motivational and self-help books flood the marketplace. But, there is only one book that tells us how to die. And, there is no one verse in that Book of Books which is more pertinent to the subject than our verse today. Tradition tells us King David penned these words about the "valley of the shadow" while sitting in the Judean wilderness between Jerusalem and Jericho. The spot is known today as

Wadi Kelt. It is a long valley about four and a half miles in length and its canyons run as much as 1500 feet in depth. The sun casts a shadow across the canyon on the sheep trails across the way which snake their way up and down and through the rugged terrain. It was here that David said, "Yea, though I walk through the valley of the shadow of death…" This one verse reveals three important facts about this appointment that awaits each and everyone of us.

FACT #1: DEATH IS A SURETY

Death is sure. It is certain. We deal with death in many ways. Some attempt to flee it. Some go to the extreme of cryonics, freezing their bodies in hopes that future medical breakthroughs can bring them back to life at some later date. Some forget it. They simply reject the idea, assuming it will somehow go away. Others fear it. Thus, they live paralyzed lives with no hope or security in Christ. Then, there are those, like David, who face it. They realize their "days are numbered" and we all have an appointment with death.

Note carefully David's words, "…I WALK through the valley…" He walked. He didn't run toward death. This is King David, not Dr. Kevorkian. He didn't crawl, as though he wanted to postpone it as long as possible. He was not dragged toward it. He simply "walked." He knew death could not be avoided, it is a surety.

FACT #2: DEATH IS A SOJOURN

David indicated that he walked "through" the valley. It

was not his final destination. It was only a temporary passage, a sojourn. He knew this road was not a dead end with no way out. He knew it was not a cul-de-sac that got him nowhere. For David, and for us, death is simply a sojourn. We do not walk "in" the valley. We do not stay there. We walk "through" the valley.

The story is told of a caterpillar crawling along a limb on his belly. A friend comes by with a philosophical view that says, "Someday I believe we will no longer crawl around like this but be able to fly and soar and feast on the milk and honey." "How idealistic," thought the caterpillar. Then, one day came his inevitable appointment with death. So he was buried in a shroud called a cocoon and attached to a twig on a tree. By and by, when spring came, the grave bursts open, and out of it emerges a magnificent creature with delicate sails called butterfly wings. In our superior intellect we know this is the process of metamorphosis. But, do we know as much about our own destinies? Death is a surety. But, it is also only a sojourn. It is not our final destination.

FACT #3: DEATH IS A SHADOW

Solomon reminds us in his Proverbs that "every word of God is pure." Note carefully what David says, "Yea, though I walk through the valley of the SHADOW of death…" No believer in Christ ever walks through the valley of death, only the valley of the shadow of death. The Lord Jesus walked through the valley of death. For three days and nights he walked that valley and then emerged from the empty tomb and said, "Behold, I now hold the keys of death and hell."

Thus, the believer only walks through the valley of the "shadow" of death. A shadow might horrify you. But, it cannot harm you. And, the only way you can have a shadow is to have a great light shining. David said he walked "through the valley of the shadow of death" because that is what we do with a shadow, we simply walk through it.

While death is a surety, it is only a sojourn through a shadow. It is, in a sense, stepping into the light. Jesus said, "I am the light of the world, he who follows Me shall not walk in darkness, but have the light of life." (John 8:12).

Is it any wonder David went on in this verse to exclaim, "I will fear no evil"? He knew death would be defeated; that although it was a surety, it was but a temporary sojourn through a shadow into the light. He could fear no evil because he knew the Lord was with him. "I will fear no evil…. for You are with me!" Up until now in this great 23rd Psalm David had been speaking in third person… "He makes me….He leads me…He restores me." But, when it comes to the subject of death he gets very up close and personal. All of a sudden, things change to second person here in verse four… "You are with me…Your rod…Your staff…You prepare…You anoint…" Death has its own way of making Christ more personal in our own experience.

No wonder we, too, can fear no evil. Why? Because the Lord is with us and He has conquered death, hell and the grave. The Apostle John got a glimpse of His glory from his lonely island called Patmos where he was exiled. Upon seeing the vision of the exalted Christ he formed it the best he could with our limited vocabulary and said, "When I saw Him, I fell at his feet as dead. But He laid His right hand on me, saying to me, Do not be afraid. I am the first and the last. I am He who lives; and was dead, and behold, I am alive forevermore. Amen. And I have the keys of Hades and of death." (Revelation 1:17-18). Yes, "though I walk through the valley of the shadow of death, I will fear no evil, FOR YOU ARE WITH ME."

As you memorize this verse, meditate on the fact that through His own death and resurrection the Lord Jesus makes a way out of no way for us. We need not fear death. We only walk through the valley of the "shadow" of death... and He is with us!

CHAPTER 39:
A Faith That Works

*"For as the body without the spirit is dead,
so faith without works is dead also" (James 2:26).*

There has always been an ongoing controversy in ecclesiastical circles over the nature of our salvation. People tend to gravitate toward one of two extreme views. One view overemphasizes faith while forgetting works; the other overemphasizes works while forgetting faith. The former is referred to as an "easy believism." Proponents of this soteriology think one can say a simple "sinner's prayer" which is not accompanied by any change of lifestyle, no prayer or Bible study and no desire for spiritual things and still be saved because he "prayed the prayer." The latter is referred to as a "works salvation." Proponents of this approach seem to think one can earn his salvation through "good works."

This conflict between faith and works is as old as the church herself. The entire argument finds its roots in the second chapter of James and in particular here in James 2:26, "Faith without works is dead." All through the Scripture the emphasis is on the fact that salvation is wholly by grace through faith in Christ Jesus alone and "not of works lest anyone should boast"(Ephesians 2:9). However, the Bible also teaches that true saving faith is always accompanied by "fruit" and will result in good works.

James reveals that a faith without fruit is a false faith (James 2:14-17), a futile faith (James 2:18-19) and a fatal faith (James 2:20-26). Many misunderstand the message of James. He is not talking about a faith *with* works, but a faith *that* works. And there is an eternity's worth of difference.

The famous reformer, Martin Luther, became so frustrated with this argument; he went so far as to refer to the Epistle of James as "an epistle of straw." But again, it is not about a faith *with* works, but a faith *that* works!

On the surface it appears to some that the message of Paul in the New Testament and the message of James are in diametric opposition to one another. For example, James asks, "Was not Abraham our father justified by works when he offered Isaac his son on the altar?" (James 2:21). Paul counters, "If Abraham was justified by works, he has something to boast about, but not before God. For what does the Scripture say? 'Abraham believed God and it was accounted to him for righteousness'"(Romans 4:2-3). However, in reality, the two do not contradict each other, they actually complement each other.

FAITH AND WORKS ACCORDING TO JAMES

Some have accused James of an attempt to answer Paul in this passage. Since James wrote his letter in 48 A.D. and Paul did not write the Roman letter until at least 58 A.D. this has no merit. James and Paul are coming at the issue from different perspectives. Paul was writing to the Judaizers who were saying that one had to add works of the law to faith in order to receive salvation. Thus his emphasis was on faith alone. He was arguing for the primacy of faith. James, on the other hand, was writing to people who went to the other extreme. They claimed to have faith but, in reality, had only intellectual assent. Therefore, his emphasis was on what Jesus called the "fruit" of our faith. He was simply arguing for the proof of faith.

FAITH AND WORKS ACCORDING TO PAUL

Paul consistently emphasized that no one enters God's kingdom except by faith and by faith alone. James is in agreement with him. He began his letter saying, "He chose to give us birth through the word of truth" (James 1:18). Here in the second chapter James is simply reinforcing the point that good works are the natural response of true saving faith. He is not saying works are the requirement for salvation, but that they are the result of our salvation.

"As the body without the spirit is dead, so faith without works is dead." It is not a faith with works at issue here, but a faith that works. Paul reminds us that "we are his workmanship, created in Christ Jesus for good works, which God has prepared beforehand that we should walk in them" (Ephesians 2:9-10). We are saved by faith alone; but faith that saves is never alone.

As you memorize this verse, meditate on the relationship between faith and works. And remember, it is a faith THAT works that pleases God.

CHAPTER 40:
Ultimate Love

"But God demonstrates His own love toward us, in that while we were still sinners, Christ died for us" (Romans 5:8).

I was a young pastor and it was a bitter cold winter afternoon. Snow and ice covered the windswept cemetery as I stood with a young couple at the open grave of their new born baby. We wept and prayed, I read Scripture, said a few words of comfort, and we left. I went home that evening and could not get that broken hearted mother and father out of my mind. They went home that same evening and began to put away the baby crib in which that little package of love had slept for the past several weeks. On impulse, I went into our firstborn daughter's room, picked her up and sat down in the den. I wondered how I would have felt had I been that other young dad who sat in his home a few blocks away. What if God had taken my child? After all, she was just a few days old and, at the time, really did not know me anymore than the man next door. I came to the conclusion that night that the thing that would have bothered me most was that she would never have really known, in this life, how much her father really loved her and was willing to give himself for her.

And, that is the tragic thing about living a life without Christ. Those who do not know Christ can never know how much the Father loves them. Our God demonstrated His love when we were least deserving. He did something. He gave us His only Son who "died for us." No wonder, the Bible says, "Greater love has no one than this; than to lay down one's life for his friends" (John 15:13).

THE PROOF OF HIS LOVE

God proved His love toward us. How? It was not by writing His love in flaming letters across the sky, nor by echoing His strong voice from heaven expressing His love. The Bible says, "When the fullness of time had come, God sent forth His Son, born of a woman, born under the law." (Galatians 4:4). Jesus was not some sort of remedial action, a sort of last-minute splint on a broken world when everything else had failed. The preparation God had done was staggering. He raised up a Greek world which spread the Greek language across the known world so that the gospel could spread without a language barrier. He raised up a Roman empire which had built a road system of 50,000 miles across the world so that the gospel could spread from country to country. Yes, it was in the "fullness of time" that Christ came.

There is something within each of us that longs to be loved. And God loves us so much that "He demonstrated His own love toward us." He sent His Son. No one in the earth has a DNA like yours. No one has a thumbprint just like yours. You are an individual, loved by the Lord. And, the love you can voluntarily return to Him is indescribably valuable to Him.

THE PHENOMENON OF HIS LOVE

The phenomenal thing about the love of God is that it is expressed to us not when we were perfect or deserving. It came to us "while we were still sinners." In fact, "Scarcely for a righteous man will one die; yet perhaps for a good man someone would even dare to die...BUT GOD demonstrates His own love toward us in that WHILE WE WERE STILL SINNERS Christ died for us" (Romans 5:7-8). Those two little words, "But God," make all the difference.

Jesus came and clothed Himself in human flesh. He became what we are so that we could become what He is. He was forsaken so that we might never be forsaken. As someone said, "The Son of God became the Son of Man in order that the sons of men could become the sons of God."

THE PRICE OF HIS LOVE

"Christ died for us." Let those words sink in for just a moment. He died your death so you could live His life. He took your sin so you could take His righteousness. "For God so loved the world HE GAVE...." For 33 years, He gave. We must have embraced and loved Him for it. Did we love Him? We hated Him. We spit in His face. We beat Him with a leather strap until His back was a bloody pulp. We stripped Him naked and mocked Him. We put a scarlet robe on Him and smashed a crown of thorns on His brow. And then we laughed…and laughed…and laughed. Then we plucked His beard out with our hands; then laughed some more. Finally, we took His hands; those same hands that once had calmed storms, stroked the children's heads, multiplied the loaves and fishes, formed the spittle for the blind man's eyes and had clasped themselves in prayer in the garden…and we nailed them fast to a cross. Then, we took those same feet that had run errands of mercy to so many, which had walked on the sea, and we nailed them to a cross.

The price He paid to "demonstrate" His love was great. Every lash of the whip, every sound of the hammer, was the voice of God saying, "I love sinners."

As I held my little daughter tight that night, I thought, "I'd give the world to her if I could." Then it occurred to me that God had said just the opposite. He said, "I'll give my Son to the world." It isn't any wonder the songwriter of old said, "Oh, the love that drew salvation's plan. Oh, the grace that brought it down to man. Oh, the mighty gulf that God did span….AT CALVARY."

As you memorize this verse, meditate on "the breadth, the length, the depth and the height" of God's love for you personally. No one else has your DNA. You are an individual, indescribably loved by Him. Let God love you today.

CHAPTER 41:
Forsaken!

"And about the ninth hour Jesus cried out with a loud voice, saying, "Eli, Eli, lama sabachthani?" that is, "My God, My God, why have You forsaken Me?" (Matthew 27:46).

During the intense struggle of the cross, our Lord spoke seven times as He hung suspended between heaven and earth. This was the strangest of all His cries, "My God, My God, why have you forsaken me?" Was He actually forsaken by the Father during His moments of agony? As the battle raged, Satan tried his best to entice Christ to give up, to give in, and to give out. On the cross he sought to get Him to give out, to call legions of angels to set Him free. This was the spiritual battle. When His disciples deserted Him, Satan tempted Him to just give in. That was the battle in the soulish realm. During the trials and beatings before the cross, the devil sought to get our Lord to give up. This was the physical battle.

Many today know the haunting feeling of being "forsaken." Some once stood at a wedding altar and heard their lover promise to "never leave or forsake." But, they lied and now they know the reality of the word, "forsaken." Countless children have been abandoned by fathers and mothers and know the meaning of the word. Perhaps there is no more haunting word in our English language than this word—"Forsaken." Let's take a brief journey with our Lord from Galilee to Gethsemane to Golgotha and learn from Him how to overcome being "forsaken."

AT GALILEE HE WAS FORSAKEN BY HIS FAMILY *(Matthew 13:53-58)*

His own brothers and sisters distanced themselves from Him when He burst forth into His public ministry. They thought, for awhile, that He was mentally imbalanced. It was at this point that He said, "A prophet is not without honor, except in his own country and in his own house" (Matthew 13:57). He had no honor "in His own house." He was forsaken by His family.

When those who knew Him best forsook Him, instead of giving up…He reached up. We read these words, "And when He had sent the multitudes away, He went up on a mountain by Himself to pray. Now when evening came, He was alone there" (Matthew 14:23). When He was forsaken by His own family, He did not give up. All "alone," He reached up to His heavenly Father. This is a challenge for all of us who know the haunting reality of being forsaken. Instead of giving up, reach up to the Lord in prayer. He is the One person who can truly identify with your feelings and needs. For, He too, knows what it is to be "forsaken."

AT GETHSEMANE HE WAS FORSAKEN BY HIS FRIENDS *(Matthew 26:36-56)*

The night He needed His friends and followers the most, immediately after He had agonized in prayer, sweating drops of blood in Gethsemane's garden, the Bible bluntly states, "Then all the disciples forsook Him and fled" (Matthew 26:56). They forsook Him. And that is not all. They fled! They ran away. They denied they had ever known Him. They fled in the darkness of the night. He was forsaken, abandoned, in His deepest hour. And, He was forsaken not by His foes, but by His own friends.

When those formerly faithful followers fled from Him, instead of giving in…He reached in. Hear Him from under the olive trees of Gethsemane, "My soul is exceedingly sorrowful, even to death…If it is possible, let this cup pass from Me; nevertheless, not as I will, but as You will" (Matthew 26:38-39). Our Lord did not give in to the circumstances that swirled around Him. He reached in; into the depths of His own being to find His solace, not in His own will, but in the will of the One who sent Him. Have you reached in lately? That is, have you come to the place in your own experience where you join Him in praying, "Not as I will, but as You will"?

AT GOLGOTHA HE WAS FORSAKEN BY HIS FATHER *(Matthew 27:33-46)*

What happened to move Him to ask, "My God, My God, why have you forsaken Me?" For hours He had hung on the cross. Then darkness enveloped the land at noonday.

There was a deathly silence. Then, a cry penetrated the darkness, "My God — Why have You forsaken Me?"

Does a loving God forsake His own? He did not forsake Daniel in the lion's den. He did not forsake the three Hebrews in the burning fiery furnace of Babylon. Then, why this strange cry from the lips of our Lord in His most agonizing moment? The Bible tells us that a holy God cannot look upon sin (Habakkuk 1:13). On the cross Jesus was bearing your sin and mine in His own body, suffering the punishment for them as though they were His own. As Isaiah said, "All we like sheep have gone astray; we have turned, every one, to his own way; and the Lord has laid on Him the iniquity of us all." (Isaiah 53:6). As Paul reminds us, "For He made Him who knew no sin to be sin for us, that we might become the righteousness of God in Him." (2 Corinthians 5:21). During the darkness, the Light turned away. There, on the cross, bearing our sin, Jesus was momentarily forsaken, in order that we might never be forsaken.

When this happened, our Lord was tempted of the devil to give out, to cry, "Enough, I quit." But, instead of giving out…He reached out. Hear Him from the cross as He reached out saying, "Father, forgive them for they do not know what they do" (Luke 23:34). Hear Him reaching out to the dying thief alongside Him, "Today, you will be with Me in Paradise." (Luke 23:43). His arms are open wide to us today. And, never were they opened wider than when they were stretched out on the cross. He did not give out. He reached out.

What about your own life journey? Have you been to Galilee; that place where you are so tempted to give up? Reach up. This is the place where you surrender yourself. Have you been to Gethsemane; that place where you are so tempted to give in? Reach in. This is the place where you search yourself. Have you been to Golgotha; that place where you are tempted to simply give out? Reach out. This is the place where, like Christ, you sacrifice yourself.

Yes, our Lord was "forsaken" by family, friends and His Father. But, only so that we might never be forsaken. "Surely He has born our griefs and carried our sorrows." What a Savior!

As you memorize this verse, meditate on the way we never experience anything in this life that He did not experience before us and for us. Forsaken? Don't give up…reach up. Don't give in…reach in. And, don't give out…reach out.

CHAPTER 42:
Ambassadors for Christ

"Now then we are ambassadors for Christ, as though God were pleading through us; we implore you on Christ's behalf, be reconciled to God" (2 Corinthians 5:20).

As believers, we have a very significant and high responsibility and assignment. We are to be ambassadors for the King of all kings. What exactly is an ambassador? He, or in many cases, she, is appointed by the President of the United States to represent the interests of our country in particular nations around the world. Since the leader of our nation cannot be in all these places, he sends a representative to live in each of the various countries in order to represent the United States. These people are called "ambassadors."

Paul says, "We are ambassadors for Christ." We are sent from heaven into this "foreign land" to be His representatives. We are to be Christ's own ambassadors on our block, in our school, at out office, and wherever we may go. In order to truly execute the duties of representing our King with honor and integrity, we should know some of the common marks of an ambassador.

AN AMBASSADOR'S CITIZENSHIP

To begin with, it should be obvious that an ambassador from the United States to a foreign nation must be a citizen of America. No alien could ever represent our nation in a distant country. None of us would expect our government to send someone from Syria to represent the United States in Egypt.

A true ambassador of Christ is one whose "citizenship is in heaven" (Philippians 3:20). Exiled on the island of Patmos, John, the Revelator said, "I was on the island that is called Patmos....but I was in the Spirit on the Lord's Day" (Revelation 1:9). John knew it was not just where he was, but whose he was that mattered most as he represented his Lord. Those who are truly Christ's ambassadors are those who have passed "from death unto life" and from "darkness into light" by trusting in Christ alone by faith for their salvation. Hence, they may reside "in the world" but they are not "of the world." They belong to another kingdom.

AN AMBASSADOR'S CHARACTER

A representative from the U.S.A. abroad must be above reproach in character. Before he is ever appointed, he goes through the closest scrutiny imaginable. His moral character, his financial dealings, his work record, his every word and deed comes under the microscope. The ambassador should be blameless in character.

Should an ambassador for the King of kings and the Lord of lords be any less? As representatives of Christ we should possess the highest moral qualities. Our reputation should be spotless and our character beyond reproach.

AN AMBASSADOR'S CONDUCT

An ambassador must not have divided loyalties or interests. He must be selfless in his approach. One who represents our country abroad must put in abeyance any conflict which might come with his assignment in any way. His conduct must be of the highest order to effectively represent the needs and concerns of our nation.

The same certainly holds true for those of us who are "ambassadors for Christ." It was at this point that the Apostle Paul said, "And He died for all, that those who live should live no longer for themselves, but for Him who died for them and rose again" (2 Corinthians 5:15). Christ expects those of us who represent Him in our world to live for Him with conduct that becomes our office.

AN AMBASSADOR'S CONSISTENCY

An ambassador must be steadfast and live with unquestioned, consistent loyalty. We would not want to have a U.S. ambassador to Russia who could not be trusted. He must be consistent in his dealings and totally loyal to his government. If not, it would be treasonous.

I wonder if there are some "ambassadors for Christ" who should be tried for treason? He saved us. He made us His own ambassadors, and yet, some of us have sided with the world's crowd. We seldom speak of His goodness to others nor represent His interests. God desires His ambassadors to be consistent in their Christian living. It is one thing to be an Ambassador from the United States to a friendly nation, like England. It is quite another, to be an ambassador in a hot spot like the Sudan. The same is true for those of us who are Christ's ambassadors in difficult places today. It takes a special person to be His ambassador in a combat zone. It demands not only pure character and proper conduct but personal consistency.

AN AMBASSADOR'S COMMUNICATION

An effective ambassador is one who has mastered the art of communication. He is in constant, daily communication with the State Department. At the same time, he constantly communicates with the nation to which he is assigned. In most situations, the ambassador is bilingual, speaking both the language of home and the native language of the country of his assignment.

Now, if we are to be effective ambassadors for Christ, we must, ourselves, be in constant, daily contact with headquarters. We must also be communicating the wishes, desires and commands of our Leader to those among whom we live. Otherwise, we have fallen short of our calling and task.

AN AMBASSADOR'S CONSIDERATION

Ambassadors are considered and chosen on the basis of their ability to be men and women of diplomacy. The art of diplomacy is high on the list of their most important objectives. They are most effective when they are winsome in the way they go about their work. We certainly would not want someone representing our nation who was abrasive and constantly agitating others.

How much more should we, as Christ's own ambassadors, be winsome in the way we go about our own work and witness. We should be the most appealing and welcoming people to be found anywhere. In fact, the Bible says we are to be "the fragrance of Christ" (2 Corinthians 2:15) to those around us.

As Christ's ambassadors, we have a single purpose. It is to "implore others on Christ's behalf to be reconciled to God." This is our assignment. This is our task. In order to accomplish it we must take on all the characteristics of an ambassador. We have been appointed by our King to be His "ambassadors." Let's make sure we live up to our calling.

As you memorize this verse, meditate on all the qualities of an ambassador and as you go about your own work and witness this week, represent Him in a manner worthy of your calling.

CHAPTER 43:
Integrity...Don't Leave Home Without It!

"He who walks with integrity walks securely, but he who perverts his ways will become known" (Proverbs 10:9).

What is the single most important trait of one who desires to truly make a difference in our world today? Some would say it is intellect. After all, knowledge is power in many ways. Others contend it is intensity, that spirit of conquest accompanied by a passion that becomes contagious. Still others suggest it is insight, good old common sense along with the ability to see through certain issues. However, I contend it is integrity. We have all known people along life's journey with incredible intellect, but no integrity, and they are no longer in the race. Others possessing amazing intensity and passion, but little integrity, have gone the same way. The same is true with insight. Integrity is our most valuable commodity.

Integrity is that state or quality of being complete; the freedom from corrupting influences or motives. The thesaurus identifies it with such words as honesty, completeness and incorruptibility. Yes, "He who walks with integrity walks securely."

Each of us lives in four distinct spheres of life and influence. You live in a private world. There is a part of you where no one really goes. Those closest to us, our husbands, our wives, do not know all our private thoughts. No one invades your private world but you…and the God who knows all your private thoughts. You also live in a personal world. This is that part of you which is shared by a small circle of immediate family and, perhaps, a very few friends who really know you intimately. Next, comes your professional world. This existence consists of dozens or even scores of men and women who, although they do not know you personally, much less privately, know you in a professional setting. Finally, you live in a public world. This is the world in which anyone who hears your name, even though they have never met you personally or dealt with you professionally, have formed an opinion of you one way or another. We call this our public persona. This brings into play an important question — where is integrity in life rooted?

INTEGRITY IS ROOTED IN THE PRIVATE LIFE

Integrity stems from an inner power, not an outer promotion. It is rooted in that private life alone with God in the secret, hidden place. We often hear architects, engineers or builders say, "This building has structural integrity." That is, the public beauty of a tall skyscraper rests upon its private, unseen foundation which is dug deep into the earth and solidly constructed. It is the hidden life of a building that brings "structural integrity." It is the hidden life of an orange tree, that unseen root system that digs deep into the earth, from which those juicy, delectable fruits emerge. And so it is with us. Integrity is rooted in the private life.

What made a man like Billy Graham so influential and so believable for so many decades? Was it his intellect? There were many much smarter than he. Was it his intensity? It was, without question, his unblemished integrity which earned him a prolonged hearing. King Solomon had it right: "The integrity of the upright will guide them…" (Proverbs 11:3).

INTEGRITY IS REFLECTED IN THE PERSONAL LIFE

Once integrity is rooted in our private life, the natural response is that it begins to be reflected in our relationships with those closest to us. Many seem to think that it is rooted in the dynamic of these close interpersonal experiences. But, it is not. It is only reflected there, if, in fact, we are men and women of integrity. If you want to know if I have integrity, ask my wife or my daughters who really know me in the intimacy of close family relationships. Integrity does not find its roots in the personal world. However, it is certainly reflected there.

INTEGRITY IS REINFORCED IN THE PROFESSIONAL LIFE

What about your professional life….that sphere of life that is ever widening? If you have a hidden life where your own integrity finds its roots, it will not only be reflected in your close relationships with those around you, it will be reinforced in your day-to-day dealings in the work world. Integrity is reinforced on the anvil of personal experience and practice in the marketplace.

Our greatest opportunity to make a difference and engage our culture is out in the marketplace. It is imperative that, as Christians, we are men and women of integrity in the professional world around us. There are a decreasing small percentage of people in our cities in church on Sunday mornings. However, on Monday, multitudes scatter into the marketplace. They take note of individuals of integrity. Integrity is not rooted in our professional life; it is only reinforced there. That is, if we truly possess it.

INTEGRITY IS REVEALED IN THE PUBLIC LIFE

Once we are thrust into the public arena, it is too late to look for integrity. If we do not already possess it, it is too late. However, some seek to put a "spin" on their personal promotion in a hopeless effort to somehow lead others to believe they are people of integrity. It is not rooted there, only revealed there if we have it or not. Solomon's words ring true today, "He who walks with integrity walks securely, but he who perverts his ways will become known."

When integrity is rooted in the private world, it is reflected in the personal world, reinforced in the professional world, and, ultimately, revealed in the public world for the glory of the God whom we love and serve.

As you memorize this verse, meditate on your own private life. Bring focus to that time alone with God, your hidden life. Then "all these other things will be added to you."

CHAPTER 44:
The Word Became Flesh

*"And the Word became flesh and dwelt among us,
and we beheld His glory, the glory as of the only begotten of
the Father, full of grace and truth" (John 1:14).*

Who is this "Word" spoken of in the opening verses of John's gospel? Was it another one of the prophets sent from God to deliver His message to us? Was it some high and holy angel who had been dwelling in the celestials for millennia? No, this "Word" is infinitely more than any of the created beings. This is God Himself, stepping out of heaven, clothing Himself in human flesh, and entering our own time warp of human history. John is explicit as to His identity;, "In the beginning was the Word, and the Word was with God, and the Word was God" (John 1:1).

Accompanying this incredible description of the incarnation of Christ are several other Christological mountain peaks of Scripture. Probing the depths of this deep truth, Paul said, "God has highly exalted Him and given Him the name which is above every name...that every knee should bow and every tongue should confess that Jesus Christ is Lord, to the glory of God the Father" (Philippians 2:9-11). To the Colossians he said that Christ "is the image of the invisible God...for by Him all things were created...and in Him all things consist...that in all things He might have the preeminence" (Colossians 1:15-18). And, the writer of Hebrews relates that "He purged our sins and sat down at the right hand of the Majesty on high." (Hebrews 1:4).

The incarnation, that period of 33 years when God invaded earth clothing Himself in flesh and bone, is one of the most condescending displays of Divine love to be found anywhere at any time. In the incarnation, we catch a glimpse of God's garment, grace and glory.

GOD'S GARMENT

The Word became flesh. Jesus came down to where we are so we could go to where He is! He came to us and took on our flesh. He was not God and man as He walked the ways of this world. He was the unique God-man. As God, He walked on water, calmed the storm, healed the sick and rose from the dead. As man, He got thirsty and tired. He felt sorrow and pain.

Think about it….He came, not clinging to all the brightness of His glory, not shunning us for our sinful conditions, but humbling Himself to become a servant and to clothe Himself in flesh. By doing so, there would not be one emotion, one temptation, one pain with which we dealt that He could not say, "I understand."

After all, if God were to become a man we would certainly expect Him to have an unusual and unique entrance into our existence. He came, not as a full grown man, but He became as helpless as a tiny seed planted in the womb of a young Jewess virgin. He came, not to be born in a clean and sterile environment on starched white sheets, but, in the dung and filth of a Bethlehem stable where sickness, disease, and even death were all likely possibilities. This is amazing condescension. He took on the garment of human flesh.

GOD'S GRACE

In the incarnation, we also see God's amazing grace. Yes, He "dwelt among us...full of grace and truth." The word translated "dwelt" means to take up temporary residence as though one lived in a tent. This was our Lord's mission. He came here, for a time, in order to pay the penalty for our sin, that He might bring us to the Father. Thus, He "dwelt among us;" but only temporarily in human flesh.

The text continues to inform us that He was "full of grace." Grace is defined as unmerited favor. Jesus was full of that. There is a difference between mercy and grace. Mercy is not getting what we do deserve. Grace is getting what we do not deserve. Jesus' love is always manifested in His grace. Consistently in Scripture we find Him extending this undeserved and unmerited favor upon sinners. Even at the cross we find Him praying for the forgiveness of those who were persecuting and killing Him. The Word, who became flesh, was "full of grace."

Our Lord was also "full of truth." In fact, He was the embodiment of truth. It is only when His grace leads us to know the truth that we are truly free. Jesus came, not to talk to us about God, but to show us what God was like so that the simplest mind might know the Father as intimately as the most intelligent academic.

GOD'S GLORY

In Christ's incarnation, we also catch a glimpse of His glory. "We beheld His glory, the glory as of the only begotten of the Father." There is little doubt that John, now an old man, was reminiscing about the Transfiguration when He penned these words. He was there, along with his brother, James, and Simon Peter, when our Lord was transfigured before them into His glorified body. He saw "His glory" alright. On that mountain John witnessed Jesus as "His face shone like the sun and His clothes became as white as light." (Matthew 17:2).

The incarnation of Christ should not be thought of as a past, historical phenomenon. In a sense, it can be a continuing recurring experience. This same Jesus who was born in Bethlehem, who took on human flesh, longs to be born again in our hearts. His desire is to take up residency in you, to dwell in your flesh today. Paul reveled in this thought when he said, "Christ in you...the hope of glory!" (Colossians 1:27). Have you personally "beheld His glory" in you?

As you memorize this verse, meditate on Christ's amazing condescension. He laid aside His glory to enter human flesh...for me...for YOU.

CHAPTER 45:
The Big Ten

*"I am the Lord your God, who brought you out of the
land of Egypt, out of the house of bondage. You shall have
no other gods before Me" (Exodus 20:3).*

There are several hundred commandments in the
Torah. But "the Big Ten" are found here in Exodus, chapter
20. We are observing an intentional and intensive assault on
the Ten Commandments in our western culture today. Any
reference to them is being systematically removed from our
public squares, our public school classrooms and almost
every other place imaginable. However, a trip to our nation's
capital finds these Ten Commandments etched in granite
on government buildings, carved in mahogany in public
libraries and even center stage on the wall above where the
Supreme Court justices hold court each day. They are living
testimonies to our founding faith and to what made this the
greatest nation on earth. They have, through the years of
our Republic, been the thread with which the fabric of our
great nation has been woven. The Ten Commandments
have served as the building blocks of most every civil and
decent society for more than 3,000 years.

We all understand the importance of rules and standards in our daily lives. Can you imagine a football game
with no sideline boundary markers? What kind of order

would there be in a game where the running back could leave the playing field, run up the stadium steps, out through the parking lot, and then enter the field from another angle and score a touchdown? Boundaries are a part of our everyday life. Home builders have building codes, boundaries, with which they must adhere. We all need absolutes. Civilized society needs boundaries in which to exist. When is a train most free? Is it most free when it is trying to run through a field; or, when it stays on the tracks that have been set out for it? The same is true with us.

Our memory verse in this chapter entails the first commandment. Why? Why not the third….or the seventh…or the tenth? It is because if we get the first one right, all the others have a way of falling into place. This includes the first four; those which have to do with our relationship with God, that is, the vertical ones. It also includes those which have to do with our relationships with others; the horizontal ones, the last six. When we give the Lord priority in our lives by putting Him in first place, we will not have difficulty with stealing or lying or adultery or any of the others. It is listed first for a very significant reason. There are four very important principles to be found in this first commandment of the "Big Ten."

PRINCIPLE #1: GOD IS PRESENT

The Ten Commandments begin with an amazing declaration, "I AM." When Moses was called by God from the burning bush to be the great emancipator of his people, he asked, "When I get back to Pharaoh, who shall I say has sent me? What is your name?" God replied, "Tell him I AM has sent you." God is ever present, from eternity past to eternity future. For a brief 33-year span in history, He stepped out of space into our empirical realm. But, He has always been and always will be, "The Great I AM."

By the time the Israelite's journey brought them to Exodus 20, they found themselves at a place where they had almost forgotten their heritage. It was there, and then, that the ever present God delivered to them His Ten Commandments and wrote them on a tablet with His own finger. He is still present today. He is not someone who simply appeared one time in history and is nowhere around today. He is still the "Great I Am."

PRINCIPLE #2: GOD IS PERSONAL

He is the Lord "YOUR God." This is singular in Hebrew, indicating that God desires a one-on-one relationship with you. Many believe the Christian life is about religion. Others think it is about ritual; that is, the performance of certain outer, perfunctory duties that accompany the faith. But, it is really about a relationship; a vital, living and personal relationship with the Lord Jesus Christ.

The purpose of the law was never to save us. It is erroneous to believe that any of us can keep all the commandments. In fact, the Scripture teaches that, if we break just one of them, we are guilty of breaking all of them. Paul, in the New Testament, said the law was simply "our tutor to bring us to Christ, that we might be justified by faith." (Galatians 3:24). The law is there to "teach" us how we all far short and how much we need a Savior. We could never save ourselves by keeping the law.

God said, "I am the Lord your God." Is He? Do you know Him in the intimacy of Father and child? Do you know Him, who to know is life and life eternal? The only way we can abide by the commandments and make them a thing of the heart is to know Him in a personal relationship. He is not just always present, He is also personal.

PRINCIPLE #3: GOD IS POWERFUL

He reminds Moses that He was the one who "brought you out of Egypt, out of the house of bondage." He was the One who sent the plagues upon Egypt. He was the One pictured in the deliverance provided by the Passover Lamb. He was the One who parted the Red Sea. He was the One who led them with a cloud by day and a pillar of fire by night. He was the One who fed them daily with manna. He was the One who brought water from the rock. How prone we all are to forget how powerful our God is, to forget all He has done for us in the past.

President Woodrow Wilson once said, "A nation which does not remember what it was yesterday does not know what it is today, nor, what it is trying to do. We are trying to do a futile thing if we do not know where we came from or what we have been about." Here in this first commandment God is encouraging us to remember what awesome things He has done for us in the past. Thus, we can have power in the present and confidence in the future.

PRINCIPLE #4: GOD IS PREEMINENT

"You shall have no other gods before Me!" He could not be more specific. He demands preeminence. Allowing Him to rule on the throne of our hearts is to be the priority of every believer's life. When this happens, when we "love the Lord with all our heart, soul and mind," we are amazed at how "all these other things" are added to us.

The ancient Hebrews had a recurring tendency of falling into polytheism; worshipping other gods. Old gods never seem to die. They simply continue to repackage themselves and show up in succeeding generations. A "god" is anyone or anything which enjoys your primary devotion. Some make a god of their possessions. There is nothing wrong with possessing things, unless, they begin to possess you. Others find their god in promiscuity. Sex has become the god many worship in our modern world. Politics is the god of some. Others bow at the altar of pleasure in our sports-mad and entertainment-crazed world. But God warns, "You shall have no other gods before Me." He must have priority over all in our lives.

Once someone approached Jesus of Nazareth and

asked Him to identify the greatest of all these command-ments. In a moment, the Ten Commandments, not to men-tion the 613 other commandments in the Torah, were re-duced down to two. He said, "You shall love the Lord your God with all your heart, with all your soul and with all your mind. This is the first and great commandment. And the second is like it: You shall love your neighbor as yourself. On these two commandments hang all the law and the prophets." (Matthew 22:37-40). There you have it; the verti-cal relationship we have with God (Exodus 20:1-11) and the horizontal relationships we have with each other (Exo-dus 20:12-17) expressed in the Great Commandment.

Let's put Christ first in our lives so that we do not join the company of those who seem to forget in time that we enjoy privileges because Christ died to win them. When Christ came, He took these commandments and made them a thing of the heart. Love is the theme, eternal theme.

As you memorize this verse, meditate on each of the Ten Commandments, one by one. And remember, that "the greatest of these is love."

CHAPTER 46:
The Model Prayer

"In this manner, therefore, pray: Our Father in heaven, hallowed be Your name" (Matthew 6:9).

There is only one thing recorded in the Bible which the apostles asked our Lord to teach them to do. After living with Him for three years, traveling over all Galilee and Judea, and eating hundreds of meals together, they only asked to be taught one thing. They never asked him to teach them to preach. They did not ask Him to teach them to evangelize or to heal the sick. The only thing they ever asked Him to teach them is recorded for us in Luke 11:1. They requested, "Lord, teach us to pray." They were smart enough to know that this was the secret of His life. They had seen Him on many occasions slip away from them into the mountain to pray. They had observed Him on occasion praying all through the night. They saw Him pray before every great undertaking and after every great accomplishment. They knew that if they could capture this secret of prayer, they would then know how to preach, to evangelize and to do any of the other necessary elements of carrying out their mission and calling in life.

Perhaps, there is no other prayer that has been recited by as many people, at as many times, in as many places, as this prayer commonly called "The Lord's Prayer." However, it should be more properly referred to as the "Model Prayer." The true Lord's Prayer is found in John 17 where we have the record of His high intercessory prayer for us on the eve of the crucifixion. This prayer, found in Matthew 6:9-13, is a model, a guide for our own prayer life. It contains a prayer for God's glory and a prayer for our good.

A PRAYER FOR GOD'S GLORY

This prayer begins with the element of *worship*— "Hallowed be Your name." The word "hallowed" means sanctified; that which is set apart. The name of the Lord is unlike any other name. It is holy. Jesus is teaching us here that prayer is to be entered into with a reverent and worshipful attitude as though we were coming to a King.

It also employs the element of *witness*—"Your kingdom come." There is a kingdom of Grace and a coming kingdom of Glory presented to us in the Bible. When we pray this prayer we are praying for those around us who have never entered His kingdom of grace through being born again. We are also joining those saints of all the ages who have looked for "our blessed hope, His glorious appearance." Jesus is coming again to set up His glorious Kingdom. Thus, we join John, as he prayed from Patmos, "Even so, come, Lord Jesus" (Revelation 22:20).

This model prayer for God's glory also entails the element of the *will*—"Your will be done." In a previous chapter we heard our Lord praying beneath those ancient olive trees of Gethsemane's garden, "Not My will, but Yours be done" (Luke 22:42). Jesus is teaching us here that we cannot come to God in prayer with a selfish spirit, bent only on our way and our will. We must come to Him humbly in a spirit of submission, joining Jesus, in praying, "Your will be done."

A PRAYER FOR OUR GOOD

The remainder of this model prayer invokes our personal petitions that result not only in His glory, but in our own good. We ask for *provision*. "Give us this day our daily bread." We are dependent upon Him to meet our basic needs of life. We cannot approach Him with an independent spirit that is self sufficient. It is also important to note it is "daily" bread at issue here. One of the reasons many believers fall to the wayside along the way is that they forget this point. The manna fell daily in the wilderness and was only edible for that day. What we take in today of the Bible, the Bread of Life, sustains us for today. As we ask Him for our provisions, remember, it is "daily bread."

There is also a petition here for *pardon*—"Forgive us our debts as we forgive our debtors." Thus, we come to Him in prayer with a penitent spirit and not just a dependent one. We cannot come to Him with unconfessed and unforgiven sin in our lives. Once again note that every word is there for a reason. We are asking Him to forgive us, "as we forgive our debtors." Do we really mean this? We need to think deeply about what we are praying here. Some are prone to say, "Well, I will forgive her, but I won't have anything else to do with her." Is that really the way we wish for God to forgive us? Think about this the next time you pray this model prayer.

We also find a petition here for *protection*—"And do not lead us into temptation, but deliver us from the evil one." We need for God to lead us. He will never lead us to do wrong. There is a difference between the temptations of life and the trials of life which come our way. Trials often come from God to teach us to stand. Temptation comes from the devil to cause us to stumble. We need God's leadership and deliverance in our daily lives.

We begin this prayer by saying, "Our Father." The foundation of all true prayers is in these first two words of the model prayer, "Our Father." If you cannot say, "Our Father," you will never have an effective prayer life. And, you cannot say "Our Father" unless you have been born into His family by trusting in His Son for your eternal life.

"Our Father." Yes, we are not beggars cowering down at some backdoor looking for a handout from some cosmic benefactor. We are children, seated at His table, "making our requests known unto Him." No wonder we are invited to come with "boldness" to His throne of grace. Prayer has a twofold purpose; it is for God's glory and our good.

As you memorize this verse, meditate on the fact that this is but a pattern for our praying. Jesus never actually told us to pray this prayer. He said, "When you pray, pray like this...in this manner pray..." It is but a model for us to follow as we join the apostles in asking, "Lord, teach us to pray."

CHAPTER 47:
A New Song of Redemption

"And they sang a new song saying, 'You are worthy to take the scroll, and to open its seals, for You were slain, and have redeemed us to God by Your blood out of every tribe and tongue and people and nation'" (Revelation 5:9).

Our limited, finite minds can scarcely grasp the thought that Christ "redeemed" us with the purchase price of His own blood. The writer of Hebrews reminds us that it is "not with the blood of goats and calves, but with His own blood He entered the most Holy Place once for all, having obtained eternal redemption." (Hebrews 9:12). Simon Peter elaborates on the point saying, "You were not redeemed with corruptible things, like silver or gold, from your aimless conduct received by tradition from your fathers, but with the precious blood of Christ, as of a lamb without blemish and without spot" (1 Peter 1:18-19).

It is no wonder we will be singing this "new song" in heaven. He alone is worthy to be the object of our worship. He is the only one who was slain and redeemed us by His own blood. This verse reveals to us the hope of redemption as well as the scope of redemption.

THE HOPE OF REDEMPTION

Our hope of being redeemed is found in Christ and in

Christ alone. As Paul said, "In Him we have redemption through His blood, the forgiveness of sins, according to the riches of His grace" (Ephesians 1:7).

Redemption is the scarlet thread that is woven throughout the entire Bible. The word, redemption, comes from *agora*, the Greek word for the marketplace. In its verb form in Revelation 5:9, it indicates that Jesus Christ entered the marketplace and purchased us out of the market to be His very own. How much do you think you are worth to Him? What would He pay for you? Our redemption had an expensive price tag affixed. The cost was Christ's own blood.

In this fifth chapter of Revelation, we come upon one of the great worship experiences of all time. What is it that gives us access into Christ's presence in worship? Is it the observance of certain religious rituals, the adoration of certain images or icons? The Bible is explicit; it is the blood of the Lord Jesus which gives us access to His throne of worship, not only in the unfolding scene in Revelation, but, in our own private devotional time as well. Our only hope of redemption is in Christ and His shed blood.

THE SCOPE OF REDEMPTION

Who is covered here in this purchase price? Is it only for those on one end of the economic or social spectrum? Is it only for those who look like we look and act like we act? The new song of heaven declares that the scope of God's redemption extends to "every tribe and tongue and people and nation." Jesus reaches out to those in the most remote tribal regions of our world. His redemption knows no language barrier. It is for every tongue. And, yes, it if for every people and every nation.

I remember vividly the first time I ever saw this word "redemption." I was about eight years of age and I desperately wanted a new baseball glove. This was in the day before we used credit cards to the extent they are used today. Most of us use those plastic cards in order to earn points so that we can acquire certain goods or services without actually having to pay cash for them. Back in the "olden days" we had what was called "S&H Green Stamps." They served the same purpose. One day while browsing through my mother's catalog, I saw a genuine leather ball glove that could be mine with two and a half books of Green Stamps. Thus, I persuaded my Mom to let me have the Green Stamps she received from grocery shopping, gasoline servicing and the like. Finally, after a few months, I had licked and stuck enough Green Stamps into my books to acquire my glove.

On a given Saturday, my Dad drove me to the southside of Fort Worth. We pulled into a parking lot adjacent to a large, white concrete block building. As we were walking into the building I noted over the door the words, "S&H Green Stamp Redemption Center." I had never seen that word, redemption, before and had no idea what it meant. Upon entering the building, I approached the counter and laid out my two and a half books of Green Stamps along with the page of the catalog with the picture of the ball glove. The lady began thumbing through each page. My heart started fluttering. What if I had skipped a page? Next, she disappeared into a back room. Minutes later she returned with a square box. She shoved it across the counter in my direction. I opened it and sure enough, there was a genuine leather baseball glove inside.

I put it on my hand and started patting the pocket with my other fist. I did this all the way home. A teenager up the street had told me that I should put some linseed oil in the pocket, wrap a ball inside and tie it off with a large rubber band at night to form the pocket. I think I actually slept with that glove the first several nights I had it. I redeemed that glove…with two and a half books of S&H Green Stamps.

And so our dear Lord one day stepped up to redemption's counter…for you. His Father sent Him. Down He came, past solar systems and constellations and through measureless space; down still farther to become as helpless as a seed planted in the womb of a young virgin girl. Down even farther to be gestated in that womb for nine months. Then, down yet farther, to be born in the dung and filth of a Bethlehem stable. Then down even farther, to go about doing good, only to be beaten and mocked, spit upon and scorned, and to finally walk up to redemption's counter. There, He put down His own blood to redeem you. Why? So

He could take you home with Him!

This is the message of the gospel. This is why we will one day join that celestial choir in singing a new song, "You are worthy...for you were slain and have redeemed us to God by your blood out of every tribe and tongue and people and nation."

As you memorize this verse, meditate on the tremendous price our Lord paid to purchase you "out of the marketplace" and take you home with Him.

CHAPTER 48:
God Calling!

"And the Spirit and the bride say, 'Come!' And let him who hears say, 'Come!' And let him who thirsts come. Whoever desires, let him take the water of life freely" (Revelation 22:17).

The Spirit of God and the Bride of Christ both beckon us to come to the Lord Jesus. The "bride" is clearly a reference to the church in the New Testament; that body of born again believers who one day will be reunited with their bridegroom, the Lord Jesus Christ. It is the supreme task of the church to call people to "come" to Christ. But this is not all. It is also the "Spirit" who says, "Come." While the church issues this outward call, the Spirit of the Living God issues the inward call to our hearts. They work in tandem. "The Spirit and the bride, say 'Come!'"

In the eighth chapter of Romans, we are introduced to a chain reaction effect. Those God foreknew, He predestined. Those He predestined, He called. Those He called, He justified. And, those He justified, He also glorified. This mysterious calling of God upon our hearts is a significant part of His total redemptive act. It is not as though we are somehow neutral in all of this and God chooses some to go to heaven and certain others to go to hell. That is a false assumption in that Scripture clearly teaches that none of us are "neutral." We are not suspended in some sort of limbo as to our own responsibility. In fact, we have all gone our own way. We have all sinned and come short of God's glory. Our salvation is wholly of grace through faith in Him alone.

Thus, we have two distinct and yet related callings; the Spirit is saying, "Come," and the church, the bride, is echoing the same call as well.

THE INWARD CALL

The Bible says that the Spirit is calling us to come to Christ. This is the inward call to our hearts. I could seek to beg you on my knees, with tears in my eyes, describing the horrors of hell and the wonders of heaven, but you would not truly come to Christ unless the Spirit was drawing you. It was our Lord, Himself, who said, "No one can come to Me unless the Father who sent Me draws Him" (John 6:44). Do you recall what the Lord said to Peter immediately after he made his great confession at Caesarea Philippi? Jesus pronounced a blessing on him and then said, "Flesh and blood has not revealed this to you, but My Father who is in heaven." (Matthew 16:17). Later Paul would add, "For as many as are led by the Spirit of God, these are sons of God" (Romans 8:14). And, to the Galatians he said that it "pleased God, who separated me from my mother's womb, and called me through His grace…" (Galatians 1:15). Not to be left out, Peter weighed in saying, "You are a chosen generation, a royal priesthood, a holy nation, His own special people, that you may proclaim the praises of Him who called you out of darkness into His marvelous light" (1 Peter 2:9). Later, in this same letter He said that the God of all grace had "called us into eternal glory." (1 Peter 3:10).

One of the most beautiful illustrations of the Sprit's calling us to Christ is found in Acts 16. Here we are introduced to a very successful business lady named Lydia. Paul was preaching and issuing the outward call and the Bible reveals that Lydia whose "heart the Lord opened" (Acts 16:14) embraced the gospel message. Yes, the Spirit speaks to our hearts with His inward call saying, "Come!"

THE OUTWARD CALL

Here is a wonderful partnership of the Spirit of God working in and through the church of the Lord Jesus Christ. God has chosen to use the church to issue the outward call to the hearts of men and women across the world. Not only does the Spirit call us to come to Christ, but "the bride says, "Come!"

This is actually what happened at the grave of Lazarus. Lazarus was one of our Lord's closest earthly friends. Many nights, the Lord had stayed in his home in Bethany. Many meals He had shared at his table along with his sisters, Mary and Martha. Now, Lazarus was dead and buried. Jesus came upon the scene and found the funeral party in deep mourning. There was the outward call. There was something for the people there to do. They were to roll away the large stone that sealed the tomb. But only Jesus could bring Lazarus life. Thus, after the stone was rolled away, He issued the inward call. Jesus spoke to Lazarus saying, "Lazarus, come forth." And He did! The church's responsibility in the outward call is to roll away the stones today. As we call people to faith, we seek to roll away stones of indifference, stones of unbelief, stones of presumption, stones of pride and stones of procrastination. Once this is done, through our apologetics and our witness, it enables men and women to be more sensitive to hearing Christ's inward call to their hearts.

My mentor and pastoral predecessor, W. A. Criswell, approached this complicated issue with a rather simplistic understanding. I often heard him say that those high and lofty theological words like election, predestination and sanctification were "up there." They belonged to God. We were to leave them there and not speculate upon them. Words such as grace and faith, repentance and the like were "down here." These are the words with which we should deal. The older I have become, the more I think he was right in his assessment. Our part is to believe and receive. For the Bible says, "As many as received Him, to them He gave the right to become children of God, to those who believe in His name" (John 1:12).

As you memorize this verse, meditate on the fact that the Spirit is calling. Listen to what the Prophet Elijah referred to as "that still small voice." It is not audible. However, when you hear it, it is much louder than that! God is calling.

CHAPTER 49:
Here Comes the Judge!

"For we must all appear before the judgment seat of Christ, that each one may receive the things done in the body, according to what he has done, whether good or bad" (2 Corinthians 5:10).

Perhaps there is no other subject relegated to the back recesses of our minds than the fact that each of us will one day stand before the Supreme Judge of all the earth. In His court there are no mistrials, no appeals, no probations, no adjudicated sentences and no hung juries. It is the one court where ultimate and perfect justice will prevail.

The subject of this final judgment is also one of the most confusing ones in all Scripture. However, when we understand that there are at least four coming judgments delineated in the Bible, it brings more focus and understanding to what lies ahead. Here comes the Judge.

THE JUDGMENT OF SIN

The first judgment related to us has already taken place. It is the judgment of the believer's sin. Jesus said, "Most assuredly, I say to you, he who hears My word and believes in Him who sent Me has everlasting life, and shall not come into judgment, but has passed from death unto life" (John 5:24). Our sins were judged in Christ as He hung on Calvary's cross. He suffered for our sins. He paid our penalty.

He took our place and bore the wrath of God's judgment of sin in His own body on the cross. As Paul indicated, "He made Him who knew no sin to become sin for us" (2 Corinthians 5:21).

God judged the believer's sin one dark day outside the city walls of Jerusalem when Christ died our death so that we could eternally live His life. It is no wonder the great Apostle Paul begins the informative eighth chapter of Romans by saying, "There is therefore now no condemnation (no judgment) to those who are in Christ Jesus…" (Romans 8:1). No condemnation! I want to shout my thanks to God for those two words which are so undeserved and unmerited. Christ died in my place and took the punishment and judgment of my sins in His own body.

THE JUDGMENT OF SAINTS

The fact that Jesus stood in our place at the judgment of sin does not mean we will not stand before Him, the righteous Judge, at the judgment of the saints. This is referred to as the Judgment Seat of Christ. It is spoken of in Paul's second Corinthian epistle, "For we must all appear before the judgment seat of Christ that each one may receive the things done in the body, whether good or bad" (2 Corinthians 5:10).

At this judgment, taking place immediately after Christ's return, our works will be judged, not our sins. They were judged at the cross. Our eternal salvation is not at issue at this judgment. Here, we believers will each give an account of ourselves before God and the degree of our rewards will be assessed and determined by the One who judges all things well. One of the most beautiful things of this judgment is that "we have an Advocate with the Father, Jesus Christ the righteous" (1 John 2:1).

Christ, our advocate, our own personal defense attorney, pleads our case before the judgment bar. The good news is that God cannot and will not see our sins through the blood of Jesus.

THE JUDGMENT OF STATES

The judgment of the states, better known as the judgment of nations, takes place at the conclusion of the period of Great Tribulation. It is this judgment the Prophet Joel alluded to when he said, "He will judge all the surrounding nations" (Joel 3:11-16). This judgment determines who will enter the millennial reign of Christ. At issue here is the treatment of Israel during the period of tribulation. Jesus said, "Inasmuch as you did it to one of the least of these My brethren, you did it to Me" (Matthew 25:40).

The Bible says that Israel is still "the apple of His eye" (Zechariah 2:8). In fact, God says of Israel and His chosen people that His "eyes and heart are there perpetually" (2 Chronicles 7:16). Those who are saved in this judgment are the "sheep" that "inherit the kingdom prepared for them" (Matthew 25:34). The lost, the "goats," are those who are "turned away into eternal punishment" (Matthew 25:46). The coming millennial kingdom of Christ will consist only of the saved at its outset.

THE JUDGMENT OF SINNERS

The Apostle John was the only one of his peers who did not meet a martyr's death. At over ninety years of age, exiled to the lonely Island of Patmos by the Romans, God opened heaven to him and showed him what was to come. John put it thus, "I saw a great white throne and Him who sat on it from whose face the earth and the heaven fled away. And there was found no place for them. And I saw the dead, small and great, standing before God, and the books were opened…and anyone not found written in the Book of Life was cast into the lake of fire" (Revelation 20:11-15). This great white throne judgment follows the thousand year reign of Christ's kingdom. Only those who have not placed their trust in Christ alone for their salvation will stand before this judgment bar.

Every lost person who has ever lived will stand before Christ to give account for their lives. The Lamb's Book of Life will be opened. This book contains the names of all those who have come to know Christ as Lord and Savior during their earthly pilgrimage. The lost who stand before God will see that there was room where their names could have been listed.

Think of the billions of people who will stand before

the great white throne. How long will it take for them to come, one at a time, to stand before God and give account for everything they have ever done? It will not matter. Time will be no more. Eternity will have begun. They will be pronounced guilty, the degree of their punishment will be determined, and they will be cast into a Godless eternity of eternal darkness forever. Lost beyond hope, lost beyond help, lost beyond time, lost beyond Christ…lost, forever lost!

Here comes the judge. Christ is coming to judge the world. Only Christ is the righteous judge. None of us can stand in judgment of anyone else's heart. Ultimately, we can rest in the reality of Genesis 18:25, "Shall not the Judge of all the earth do right?"

When all is said and done, the only question that really matters in this world, and the next, is this one — Is your name in the Book?

As you memorize this verse, meditate on the wonderful privilege we, as believers, have in Christ, our Advocate. And ask yourself the question — Is my name in the Book?

CHAPTER 50:
Heaven

"For our citizenship is in heaven, from which we also eagerly wait for the Savior, the Lord Jesus Christ" (Philippians 3:20).

We live in a world where an increasing number of people do not believe in an eternal hell, a place of everlasting punishment. A Universalist mentality is the natural product of our pluralistic society. A frequently asked question is, "How could a loving God allow anyone to go to hell? My problem has always been just the opposite. By that I mean, I have no problem believing in hell. But, how could there be such a wonderful place like heaven? How could the love and grace of God be so awesome as to make it possible for a sinner like me to spend eternity in such a place?

John saw "a door standing open into heaven" (Revelation 4:1) from his lonely rock island of exile called Patmos. God has left us a few open doors in Scripture though which we can catch a glimpse of what awaits us there. Let's take a look into what lies ahead for those who trust in Him.

HEAVEN IS A PLACE OF REALITY

It is real. Throughout time God has implanted within the soul of man a longing for such a place. All primitive people believed in an afterlife. In ages gone by, the ancient cave dwellers depicted such in paintings on the walls of their caves. More than 3,000 years ago the Egyptians buried their Pharaohs with supplies, eating utensils, weapons and even servants in their quest for a life that is beyond this one. The American Indians had their "happy hunting grounds" where they believed the departed lived again. God has implanted and instilled within the very being of man a desire for another life.

This is true today. Every time a scientist enters his or her laboratory with a controlling motivation driving them to find a cure for cancer or AIDS, it is an expression of a subconscious hunger for a world that is free of pain and disease. Heaven is such a place. Every social worker sincerely motivated to abolish rancid living conditions has a subconscious longing for a world without poverty and displeasure. Every environmentalist moved to clean and purify the environment is on a quest for a type of life that is pure and beautiful. Statesmen who sit around peace tables in hot spots of our world are simply in search of a world without war and conflict.

The human soul needs heaven and it alone can finish what we leave unfinished here. Sir Isaac Newton whose mind, as has been said, could master the most profound truths as easily as most of us can master our ABCs once said, "I seem to be only a boy picking up a few small pebbles along the shore while the vast ocean of truth lies unexplored before me."

Heaven is real. It is a place. Jesus said, "I go to prepare a place for you." (John 14:2). It is a real, tangible place.

HEAVEN IS A PLACE OF RADIANCE

It is not simply a place; it is a "prepared place" (John 14:2). It is beautiful. God loves beauty or He would never have made things on this sin-cursed earth so beautiful. John got a glimpse of it one day and wrote down a few simple symbols which our poor finite minds could understand and said, "Its wall was of jasper, and the city was pure gold, like clear glass" (Revelation 21:18). It is no wonder that earlier the Apostle Paul had said, "Eye has not seen, nor ear heard, nor have entered into the heart of man the things which God has prepared for those who love Him" (1 Corinthians 2:9). Could it be that heaven is "like clear glass" because there will be nothing to hide there?

Heaven is a place of unparalleled beauty and radiance. The Revelation is filled with description after description of its glory. Time nor space nor human vocabulary permits us to attempt an explanation of its radiance.

HEAVEN IS A PLACE OF REST

So much of life is filled with exhaustion, mourning, struggles and pressures of all kinds. When we walk down those golden streets we will never see a hospital. There will be no more sickness. We will never see a counseling center. There will be no more depression or mental illness. We will never see a funeral home. There will be no more death there. We will never see a policeman in uniform or a police station. There is no crime there. There will be no court houses on the square. There will be no lawsuits and no one seeking to cheat anyone else out of something which is rightfully theirs. We will never hear the shrill sound of an ambulance siren. There will be no more emergencies. We will never have to lock our homes or look behind to see who is following us as we walk along. There will be no more fear. We will never see a handicapped parking place or a ramp for a wheelchair. There will be no nursing homes there for we will never grow old. Heaven is a place of rest.

There are several "no mores" in heaven. No more death. No more tears. No more mourning. No more crying. No more pain. No more farewells. No more separation. No more sorrow. No more sin. Whatever it is that may rob the joy out of life in this world will be gone and gone forever. Heaven is a place of rest.

HEAVEN IS A PLACE OF RECOGNITION

We will know each other in heaven. If fact, the Bible says we will be known as we are known. When Peter, James and John stood with Christ on the Mount of Transfiguration, Moses and Elijah appeared before them in their glorified forms and were readily recognized. No one will have to introduce me to Paul or Peter or anyone else. And, these heroes of the faith will know you and me. It is one thing for us to know the President of the United States, but it is quite something different for him to know us, to call us by name. In heaven we will know and be known.

Recently a NASA scientist speculated about the possibility of "alien" life on other planets. I have news for him. There is alien life on our planet. Those of us who are Christians are aliens in this world for "our citizenship is in heaven." We are citizens of another kingdom. We are simply passing through on our way home.

HEAVEN IS A PLACE OF REWARD

The Bible speaks repeatedly of certain crowns which will be given believers as rewards in heaven. There is the "crown of righteousness" which is given to those who live godly lives and anxiously "love His appearing." (2 Timothy 4:7-8). There is also the "crown incorruptible" which will be presented to those who run the good race and finish strongly in the Christian faith. (1 Corinthians 9:24-27). Next, there is the "crown of life." This crown is also referred to as the martyr's crown and is given to those who undergo severe trials and even death on Christ's behalf and in His service. (Revelation 2:10). There is also the "crown of rejoicing," known as the soul winner's crown. This reward is given to those men and women who are instrumental in leading other people to faith in Christ. (1 Thessalonians 2:19-20). Finally, there is the "crown of glory" given to faithful pastors and teachers who teach God's Word to others in truth and faithfulness (1 Peter 5:1-4).

These crowns are not to be worn by us as we strut up and down the streets of heaven. In one of the most humbling and beautiful scenes yet to unfold, we will take our crowns and cast them at Christ's feet. He alone is worthy to receive "power and riches and wisdom, and strength and honor, and glory and blessing!" (Revelation 5:12).

Many seem to have the idea that heaven is a long way off. Not really. It is only one heartbeat away. James asked, "What is your life?" Then, he answered his own question by indicating that life is really just a vapor. It appears for a little while and then vanishes away. For each of us, one of these days that old heart is going to stop. Then, in the wink of an eye, we will begin eternity...somewhere. Ten thousand years from today you will be alive....somewhere. Heaven awaits all who have come to God by faith alone in Christ. Jesus is the way, the only way, to the Father's house.

As you memorize this verse, meditate on the fact that your citizenship is in heaven. As the old spiritual attests, "This world is not my home, I'm just passing through." Who wouldn't want to live in such a place . . . forever?

CHAPTER 51:
Famous Last Words

"He who testifies to these things says, 'Surely, I am coming quickly.' Amen. Even so, come Lord Jesus!" (Revelation 22:20).

The final words spoken by men and women are always intriguing. Here, we have in one verse, the last promise of the Bible from the lips of Christ, and the last prayer of the Bible from the lips of John. When, after His earthly mission, our Lord ascended back to the Father, two angels appeared to his followers saying, "Men of Galilee, why do you stand gazing up into heaven? This same Jesus, who was taken up from you into heaven, will so come in like manner as you saw Him go into heaven." (Acts 1:11). Now, on the last page of the Bible, Jesus closes this Book of all books with the identical theme. This "same Jesus" promises, "Surely, I am coming quickly." And each generation following has been looking for "our Blessed Hope"; His glorious appearing.

The Bible speaks of three major comings. First, there are mentions laced through the Scriptures foretelling the first coming of Christ, born of a virgin in the seemingly insignificant little obscure village of Bethlehem. He came and "dwelt among us." For 33 years He showed us a picture of true love. However, many did not recognize Him. They thought, at best, He was "just another one of the prophets."

Next, there is the coming of the Holy Spirit foretold

especially by the prophet Joel. This took place on the day of Pentecost when the Holy Spirit came to indwell the believer, never to leave him, empowering him for service. In the old dispensation, the Holy Spirit came upon people but when they became unfaithful, He left them. One of the saddest verses of Scripture is when the Bible reveals that the Holy Spirit "departed" from Samson. King David in his prayer of repentance in Psalm 51, prayed, "Do not take Your Holy Spirit from me." But, today, in this dispensation of grace, no believer need ever pray that prayer. When we come to know Christ the Holy Spirit comes to reside in us, along with the promise that He will never leave us. As with the first coming of Christ, when the Holy Spirit came in this manner, many did not recognize Him. They accused those filled with the Spirit at Pentecost of being "drunk with wine."

The only major coming waiting to be fulfilled is the return, the second coming of Jesus Christ. Just as surely as He came the first time, He is coming again. He is coming for His bride, the church. And when He reappears, all believers will recognize Him for who He is, our coming King. The Bible indicates that no one knows when, "the day or the hour," our Lord will return. However, like with the other two major comings, there are signs, indications that this great event may be drawing near.

THE LAST PROMISE OF THE BIBLE

There are thousands of promises in the Bible. But the

last one left for us is one with a major emphasis. Jesus said, "Surely, I come quickly." Are there any indications around us which may point to this, the greatest event yet to happen in human history? While no one can speculate as to an exact time, there are several events which will herald His return.

We are to watch for a *polluted pulpit*. The Bible says that one of the sure signs that His coming is near is a turning away from the truth in the churches. Paul said, "The time will come when they will not endure sound doctrine…they will turn their ears away from the truth" (2 Timothy 4:2-4). We live in such a day when denominations are dying and Jesus is not preached as "the way, the truth and the life" any longer in many pulpits.

We are to watch for a *particular place*. Before Christ returns the Bible says that the little nation of Israel will, once again, become a major player on the world stage. God promises that He will "bring back the captives of My people Israel" into their homeland (Amos 9:14-15). Our generation has seen the miracle of the rebirth of the State of Israel. For the first time since the days of Nebuchadnezzar and the Babylonian captivity they are ruling their own country from their capitol of Jerusalem. After 2500 years of exile I have witnessed this miracle with my own eyes in my generation.

We are to watch for a *peculiar people*. Moses, long ago, predicted that "the Lord will scatter you (the Jews) among the peoples" and that they would find no "resting place" in the world. (Deuteronomy 4:27; 28:37, 65). But, Ezekiel talked of a day when God would "gather (His people) from all the countries and bring them back into their own land." (Ezekiel 36:24). While there is legitimate debate as to whether the present secular Zionist state is the Biblical Israel to come, the fact remains that unusual things are happening among this "peculiar people," the Jews.

We are to watch for a *powerful politic*. The Bible indicates that before the return of Christ a powerful coalition of nations will emerge in Europe out of the ruins of the old Roman Empire. Daniel referred to this as "the ten horns" of the ancient Roman Empire. (Daniel 7:15-25). From this new "world order" will emerge a one world government with a common currency. This seems to be happening before our very eyes.

We are to watch for a *popular politician*. Shortly before the return of Christ an electrifying leader will emerge on the world scene. He is called the Antichrist (John 2:18). This charismatic leader will promise a world of peace. He will promise to free the world of war and to bring about solutions to the world's economic and political problems. Much of the world will follow him.

We are to watch for a *pluralistic philosophy*. The Bible predicts that a new religion will emerge and seek to unite the world under one banner. A new age of humanistic thought will seek to exalt man over Christ. Every time I see a new age "crystal" hanging from a rearview mirror, I want to join John in praying, "Even so, come Lord Jesus."

THE LAST PRAYER OF THE BIBLE

Having heard this amazing promise, John's first impulse is to burst out in prayer, "Even so, come Lord Jesus!" Just five words. Often some of the most powerful prayers are the shortest ones. In this prayer John is anticipating the return of the Lord which will usher in a new age of peace followed by the endless ages of eternity.

We will never know peace internationally until we have peace on a national level. This will never happen until we have peace on a state level. We will never see peace in our state until we have peace in our city. Consequently, peace will never come to our city until it comes to my street. This is impossible unless we have peace on my block. We will never have peace on my block until we have peace in my own home. And no true peace will exist in my home unless I have found peace in my own heart through knowing the Prince of Peace Himself. Jesus is coming again to bring a kingdom of true and lasting peace among us. Join me, in joining John, praying, "Even so, come Lord Jesus!"

As you memorize this verse, meditate on this awesome event yet to come. And, examine your life to make sure you are ready and will not be ashamed at His coming. "Surely, I am coming quickly. Even so, come Lord Jesus!"

CHAPTER 52:
The Fear Factor

"Let us hear the conclusion of the whole matter:
Fear God and keep His commandments, for this
is man's all" (Ecclesiastes 12:13).

We have come now to the end of a volume. It is fitting that here we hear the words of Solomon, the wisest man who ever lived, inspired of the Holy Spirit say, "Let us hear the conclusion of the whole matter." Now, this should make us perk up our ears. Thus comes, in his words, "the conclusion of the whole matter." And here it is — "FEAR GOD!' "Fear God and keep His commandments, for this is man's all."

We live in what might be called a "no fear culture" today. We have raised a couple of generations with virtually no moral absolutes, thus relativism rages in our society. Hence, young people live with no fear. There is even an apparel company which markets to this philosophy. Their caps and shirts simply carry a logo that says, "No Fear." Unfortunately, instead of the church influencing the culture, the culture often influences the church. Thus, we awake to discover that the subject of the "fear of the Lord" has become a forgotten concept in many places of worship. How long has it been since we have heard a sermon, or given conscious expression ourselves to "the fear of the Lord"? It is as though, Isaiah was asking us and not simply his own culture, "Is there any among you who fears the Lord any-more?" (Isaiah 50:10).

A "WHY" QUESTION

Why are so many believers today living in a "no-fear culture"; where the fear of the Lord is a forgotten topic? Could it be we have lost a sense of the holiness of our God? When Isaiah received the vision of the holiness of God he said, "Woe is me." When John saw the Lord in His glory, he said he fell down at his feet like "a dead man."

All through the Bible, the common characteristic of those used of the Lord was this concept of "living in the fear of the Lord." All the Old Testament saints walked in the fear of God. Noah was "moved with godly fear" when he built the ark (Hebrew 11:7). The secret of the Proverbs 31 lady was that she was a woman "who feared the Lord' (Proverbs 31:30). Neither time nor space permits us to talk of all them. The same is true in the gospels. The young, virgin Mary sang in her song of praise, we call the Magnificat, that His "mercy was on those who feared Him." (Luke 1:50). It is on most every page in Acts. At Pentecost we read that "fear came upon every soul and many wonders and signs were done through the apostles" (Acts 2:38). Paul's epistles are replete with this same theme. To the Romans he says. "Stand by faith, do not be haughty, but fear God" (Romans 11:20). In Ephesians 5:21 he states, "Submit to one another, in the fear of God." And, finally, in the last book of the Bible, as the final scene of heaven is revealed, John says a loud voice from the throne says, "Praise our God, all you His servants, you who fear Him both small and great" (Revelation 19:5).

Thus, we are confronted with a "why" question. Why, when all those Old Testament saints, all those throughout the gospels, all those in Acts, all through the epistles instructing us in this dispensation of grace, and finally, when we get to heaven is the constant theme of all God's people this subject of "the fear of the Lord"; why is it a forgotten subject today? Have we lost a sense of the holiness of God ourselves?

A "WHAT" QUESTION

What does it mean to live in the fear of God? Does it mean we have to live in constant fright or constant flight; afraid that if we say something or do something wrong, that God will hit us with a big club of retribution? Nothing could be farther from biblical reality. The most common Old Testament word means "to stand before God with reverence and respect." The most common New Testament word is closely akin to this. It speaks of a "reverential awe" that becomes the controlling motivation of our lives.

Long years ago, as a young believer, my pastor taught me to "walk in the fear of God." It wasn't that God was going to put His strong hand of discipline on me. The fear of God is not that He will put his hand ON me; but, it is the fear that He might take His hand OFF me. It is to abide in the environment that you do not want to do anything that might cause God to take His hand of blessing or anointing off you! When we begin to live with this conscious thought it will make an incredible difference in our lifestyles as we walk "in the fear of God."

A "HOW" QUESTION

Finally, how can we put a handle on biblical truth and begin living in the fear of the Lord ourselves? Where do we begin? We begin at the place where we begin everything in the Christian life, the Word of God. Solomon frames the subject best as God speaks through him directly to us — "If you receive my words...treasure up my commandments... incline your ear to wisdom...apply your heart to under-standing...cry out for discernment...lift up your voice for understanding...seek her as silver...search for her as for hidden treasures...THEN YOU WILL UNDERSTAND THE FEAR OF THE LORD" (Proverbs 2:1-5).

In your normal traffic pattern of devotional Bible read-ing begin to circle the idea of "the fear of the Lord" every time you see it. You will be amazed how God will continue to bring it before you. Then, you will begin the journey of walking in the fear of the Lord. It is a learned experience.

Yes, when the wisest man who ever lived, inspired by God's Spirit Himself, says, "Let us hear the conclusion of the whole matter," it should make us perk our ears. "Fear God... and keep His commandments, for this is man's all."

As you memorize this verse, take your concordance and meditate on the references to the "fear of God" you will find there. And, along the way, remember the fear of God is not the fear that He might put His hand of retribution ON you; but, the fear that He might take His hand of blessing and anointing OFF you. "Is there any among you who fears the Lord anymore?"

THE GIFT OF ETERNAL LIFE

It may be that in reading this book God's Spirit is leading you to put your faith and trust in Jesus Christ alone for eternal life. Heaven is God's free gift to you and cannot be earned nor deserved. Yet, we are sinners and have all fallen short of God's perfect standard for our lives. He is a God of love and does not want to punish us for our sins but He is also a God of justice and must punish sin.

This is where the Lord Jesus steps in. He is the infinite God man who came to take our sins in His own body on the cross. He "became sin for us that we might become the righteousness of God in Him." However, it is not enough to simply know all these facts; we must individually transfer our trust from ourselves and our own human effort to Christ alone and put our faith in Him for our own personal salvation.

The Lord Jesus said, "Behold, I stand at the door and knock and if anyone hears my voice and opens the door I will come in to him" (Revelation 3:20). If you would like to receive the free gift of eternal life through Jesus Christ, call on Him, right now. He has promised that "whoever calls on His name can be saved." The following is a suggested prayer:

Dear Lord Jesus:

I know I have sinned and do not deserve eternal life in and of myself. Thank you for dying on the cross for me. Please forgive me of my sin and come into my life right now.

I turn to you and place all my trust in you for my eternal salvation. I accept your free gift of eternal life and forgiveness right now. Thank you for coming into my life.

If this prayer is the desire of your heart, you can claim the promise Jesus made to those who believe in Him — "Most assuredly I say to you, he who believes in Me has eternal life" (John 6:47).

You can now join millions of Christ's followers in saying, "You and you alone are the one and only Christ, the savior of the world and the lover of my soul." Tell someone what you have just done in receiving Christ as your own personal Savior!

ABOUT GUIDESTONE FINANCIAL RESOURCES

Dallas-based GuideStone Financial Resources is a leading financial services provider of retirement, investment and life and health plans. Operating as a church benefits board, the multibillion dollar organization is dedicated to providing outstanding products and high-touch customer service to Southern Baptist and other evangelical churches, ministries and institutions.

GuideStone offers a wide array of retirement services including retirement and executive compensation plans, personal and institutional investment products and record-keeping services. Christian-based, socially-screened investment programs utilize a sophisticated manager-of-managers philosophy. Life and Health products made available through GuideStone include a variety of term life, accident, disability, medical and dental plans with a wide range of benefit options. Property and Casualty insurance is made available to churches and ministry organizations to assist them in managing risk.

Founded in 1918 as a relief organization, GuideStone continues its tradition of providing financial assistance to retired Southern Baptist ministers and ministers' widows with insufficient retirement income. For more information about GuideStone's products, services and endowment opportunities, visit *www.GuideStone.org* or call toll-free at **1-888-98-GUIDE** (1-888-984-8433).